Bear's Paw

NEW QUILTS
from an
OLD FAVORITE

American Quilter's Society

P. O. Box 3290 • Paducah, KY 42002-3290
www.AQSquilt.com

Located in Paducah, Kentucky, the American Quilter's Society (AQS) is dedicated to promoting the accomplishments of today's quilters. Through its publications and events, AQS strives to honor today's quiltmakers and their work and to inspire future creativity and innovation in quiltmaking.

EDITOR: BARBARA SMITH & MARJORIE L. RUSSELL
GRAPHIC DESIGN: LYNDA SMITH
COVER DESIGN: MICHAEL BUCKINGHAM
PHOTOGRAPHY: CHARLES R. LYNCH

Library of Congress Cataloging-in-Publication Data

Bear's paw / [Barbara Smith, editor].
   p. cm. -- (New quilts from an old favorite)
  ISBN 1-57432-756-9
1. Patchwork--Patterns. 2. Quilting--Patterns. 3. Patchwork
quilts--Competitions--United States. I. Smith, Barbara, 1941- II.
American Quilter's Society. III. Series.
  TT835 .B293 2001
   746.46'041--dc21

                        2001001069

Additional copies of this book may be ordered from the American Quilter's Society, PO Box 3290, Paducah, KY 42002-3290, or online at www.AQSquilt.com.

This book is dedicated to all those who view a traditional quilt block and see within it a link to the past and a vision for the future.

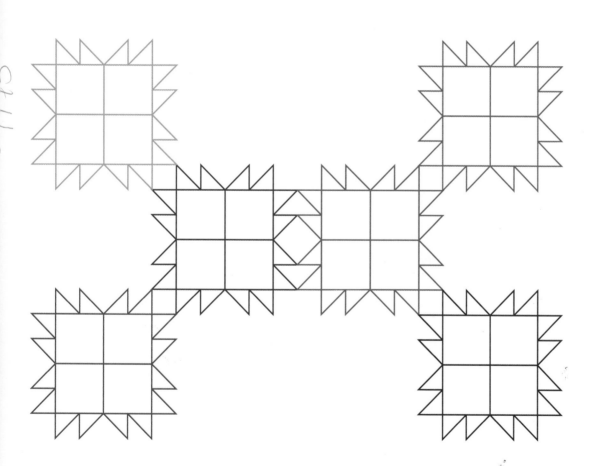

Bear's Paw: New Quilts from an Old Favorite

Contents

Techniques and Essays

Patterns

More Bear's Paw Blocks

Bear's Paw Variations

The role of a museum is not only to preserve the past. Its highest service is performed as it links the past to the present and to the future.

With that knowledge at heart, annually the Museum of the American Quilter's Society (MAQS) sponsors a contest and exhibit called *New Quilts from Old Favorites*.

Created to acknowledge our quiltmaking heritage and to recognize innovation, creativity, and excellence, the contest challenges today's quiltmakers to interpret a single traditional quilt block in a work of their own design. Each year contestants respond with a myriad of stunning interpretations.

Bear's Paw: New Quilts from an Old Favorite is a beautiful case in point. In this book you'll find a brief description of the 2001 contest, followed by a presentation of the 18 finalists and their quilts, including the five award winners.

Full-color photographs of the quilts accompany each quiltmaker's comments – comments that provide insight into their widely divergent creative processes. Full-sized templates for the traditional Bear's Paw block are included to form the basis for your own interpretation. Tips, techniques, and patterns contributed by the contest winners offer an artistic framework for your own work.

Our wish is that *Bear's Paw: New Quilts from an Old Favorite* will further our quiltmaking heritage as new quilts based on the Bear's Paw block are inspired by the outstanding quilts, patterns, and instructions in this book.

Quality Polyester Products for Home and Industry

marcusbrothers
TEXTILES INCORPORATED

JANOME

Because You Simply Love To Sew™

Bear's Paw: New Quilts from an Old Favorite

Annually, the MAQS contest, *New Quilts from Old Favorites*, challenges quiltmakers to create innovative quilts from a single traditional block pattern. The choice for millennium year 2001 was the Bear's Paw block.

Although the contest encouraged "outside the box" creativity, there were some basic requirements for entries.

- Quilts entered in the contest were to be recognizable in some way as being related to the Bear's Paw block.
- The finished size of the quilt was to be a minimum of 50" in width and height but could not exceed 100".
- Quilting was required on each quilt entered in the contest.
- A quilt could be entered only by the person(s) who made it.
- Each entry must have been completed after December 31, 1995.

To enter the contest, each quiltmaker was asked to submit an entry form and two slides of their quilt – one of the full quilt, and a second of a detail from the piece. In the *Bear's Paw* contest, quiltmakers from around the world responded to the challenge.

Three jurors viewed dozens of slides, deliberating over design, use of materials, interpretation of the theme, and technical excellence. Eventually they narrowed the field of entries to 18 finalists who were invited to submit their quilts for judging.

With quilts by the 18 finalists assembled, three judges meticulously examined the pieces, evaluating them again for design, innovation, theme, and workmanship. First through fifth place award winners were selected and notified.

Each year the *New Quilts from Old Favorites* contest winners and finalists are featured in an exhibit that opens at the Museum of the American Quilter's Society in Paducah, Kentucky. Over a two-year period, the exhibit travels to a number of museums across North America and is viewed by thousands of quilt enthusiasts. Corporate sponsorship of the contest helps to underwrite costs, enabling even smaller museums across the country to display the exhibit.

Also, annually the contest winners and finalists are included in a beautiful book published by the American Quilter's Society. *Bear's Paw: New Quilts from an Old Favorite* is the eighth in the contest, exhibit, and publication series. It joins the following other traditional block designs used as contest themes: Double Wedding Ring, Log Cabin, Kaleidoscope, Mariner's Compass, Ohio Star, Pineapple, and Storm at Sea.

For information about entering the current year's *New Quilts from Old Favorites* contest, write to MAQS at PO Box 1540, Paducah, KY, 42002-1540; call (270) 442-8856; or visit MAQS online at www.quiltmuseum.org.

There are perhaps only a handful of quilt block designs that evoke the images inspired by the Bear's Paw.

From our ancestral grandparents who could read warning or promise in a bear's footprint, to today's environmentalist who treasures the same as a symbol of earth stewardship, the Bear's Paw pattern is unmistakable in its associations. It is about bears, those hefty creatures that inspire awe, respect, and sometimes fear. Even the sharp-edged geometric shapes of the Bear's Paw block pattern lend themselves to interpretations of "bearish" attributes – dominance, presence, beauty, strength – and of the order of nature itself.

Creating a quilt with Bear's Paw as the inspiration begins, as does any artistic work, from the perspective of the quiltmaker. Endless interpretations await. Yet the basic Bear's Paw pattern is quite simple. Pieces can be quickly cut by using four simple templates or by employing rapid rotary cutting techniques. Straight piecing is also easy by machine or hand.

The winners and finalists in the *Bear's Paw* contest artistically demonstrate that a shared tradition is only the beginning. They prove that, through variations of color, theme, and innovative design, the possibilities offered by the traditional Bear's Paw pattern are limited only by the imagination.

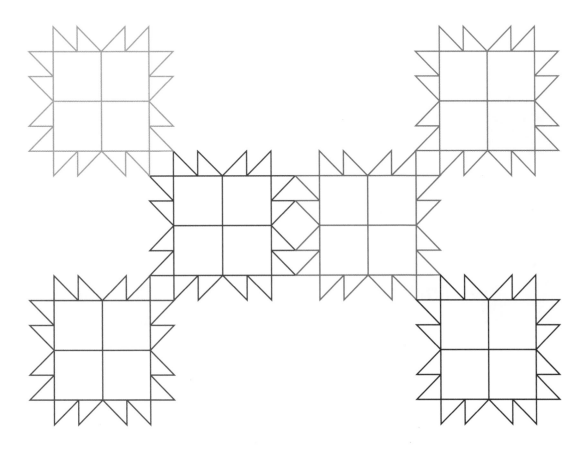

Bear's Paw: New Quilts from an Old Favorite

1st Place

Wild and Wooly
Claudia Clark Myers
Duluth, MN

2nd Place

A Night to Remember
Gayle Wallace
Taylor, LA

Gertrude Embree
Shreveport, LA

3rd Place

Vanishing
Vicky Lawrence
Overbrook, KS

4th Place

Pointed Paws
Mary Ann Herndon
Houston, TX

10

5th Place

**Last Breath of Spring
– Greenwood Ridge**
Laura Fogg
Ukiah, CA

The Bear and the Boy – I Spy the Disappearing Bear's Paw
Wendy Butler Berns

Buggy Wheels
Barbara Clem

Sammamish
Nancy Cluts

Golden Blocks and the Three Bears
Pat Cochran

Lone Bear
Sherri Bain Driver

Bears Examination
Bonnie Fredrick

Bear's Pause
Chris Lynn Kirsch

Bear Country
Fay Pritts

Oblique
Elizabeth Rymer

Bear Necessity
Judy Sogn

Investment Journey
STASH Investment and Quilting Group

Sun Paws
Cherie St. Cyr & Susan Marks

Brown Bear
Joan Walker

Bear's Paw: New Quilts from an Old Favorite

Wild and Wooly

78" x 78"

Bear's Paw: New Quilts from an Old Favorite

My workshop looks like a monsoon has struck, and the floor is littered with little trial pieces of rejected fabric, like confetti.

Meet the quilter

I think about a project for weeks before starting it. The hard part is getting the finished product to match the image in my mind. I spend so many hours rooting through my fabric, I've developed a permanent squint. My friends say I am no fun to fabric shop with. I work my way from one side of the quilt shop to the other, methodically looking at every piece of fabric and tune out shouts of "Hey, Claudia, come and look at this."

I work best with a full-sized paper version of my project on the design wall. As I piece the blocks or segments from fabric, they are pinned over the paper version on the wall. Then I stand way back to see if it looks as envisioned. Sometimes, at night, I even go outside and look at a project through the window. This vantage point has probably contributed to my style, which I call "bank lobby quilts," because many are overpowering up close.

I agonize my way through the entire process, changing fabrics and adding designs until the quilt finally looks right. I am constantly amazed by quilters who decide on a pattern, buy the exact yardage, and construct their quilts exactly as they planned. I'm glad there is room for all of us, no matter how we accomplish our goals.

Inspiration and design

There is a new Alaskan brown bear at the Duluth Zoo. He is evidently a very social bear because twice he left his home in the wilds of Denali and broke into the Anchorage Zoo, earning his name "Trouble." Our zoo's grizzly bear, Fozzie, recently died, so Duluth offered to give Trouble a new home. He was tranquilized and flown here, where his story made the papers for several days. What a coincidence, just when I needed inspiration for the Bear's Paw contest. I made plans to visit the zoo and take photos of the newest resident. However, Fozzie's longtime lady friend didn't seem to be taking to the new kid, so they couldn't move him into the bear habitat where he could be viewed by the public. Trouble was in quarantine.

While waiting for him to be available for viewing, I drafted the repeated block for the background. Using a curved ruler, I redrafted the background block and the sashing that usually completes the four-block set, to make the undulating design in the foreground. Still no Trouble, and with only six weeks to deadline, I had to make the quilt or forget it. Because time was so short and there were so many curves to be dealt with, I used a method of curved piecing combined with fused appliqué. The background was paper pieced and entirely put together, including the borders and the "X" of the center background fabric, before the curved foreground design was machine appliquéd to it. At this point, the quilt was finished and images of bears didn't seem needed.

Now, Trouble is out of quarantine and doing fine, and I believe my quilt is the better for leaving him out of it. But, thanks for the inspiration, big guy!

Curved block construction

For this quilt, a complicated curved design needed to be pieced in a short period of time. I decided to partially appliqué it by using fusible web. A master draft was made of the curved Bear's Paw block. With a fine marker, the master draft was traced on template plastic, but without the diagonal lines for the triangles. I numbered the pieces, starting with the smallest paw and working toward the largest, and lettered the pieces from left to right. Hash marks were added across the seams that would be sewn together, to help with placement (Figure 1).

I worked on one block at a time to avoid confusion. The plastic template was cut apart, and the pieces were turned face down and traced on the wrong side of the fabrics. The letter-number designation was

written on the back of each piece. I cut out each fabric patch, adding a ¼" seam allowance by eye. Then the seam lines were pinned together, starting at the corners and clipping and easing as needed, as for hand piecing. Working from the smallest paw to the largest, I sewed the seams by machine, stopping ¼" from each end, leaving the seam allowances unsewn. The outside strips were added last. All 16 blocks were sewn this way.

To add the triangles, the master pattern was again traced on template plastic, but this time, only the claw triangles were traced (Figure 2). Number-letter designations were added as before, and the triangle templates were cut apart.

Large enough fabric pieces were fused to fusible webbing so that the triangles for all 16 blocks could be cut. Then, paw by paw, I turned the templates over and drew

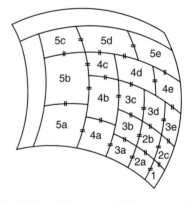

Fig. 1. *Trace the master draft on template plastic, but leave out the diagonal lines.*

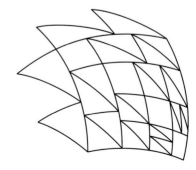

Fig. 2. *Trace the claws on template plastic.*

Bear's Paw: New Quilts from an Old Favorite

around them on the web side of the fused fabrics. No seam allowance was added this time, but the numbers and letters were written on the back of each triangle.

I cut all the 2a triangles at the same time and fused them on the 16 blocks. Then I cut all the 2c triangles, fused them, and continued in this manner, paw by paw, until all the triangles had been placed. Because the triangles were custom-trimmed before being fused to the blocks, they fit perfectly and looked as if they had been pieced. If desired, the raw edges could be covered with a narrow zigzag stitched in matching thread.

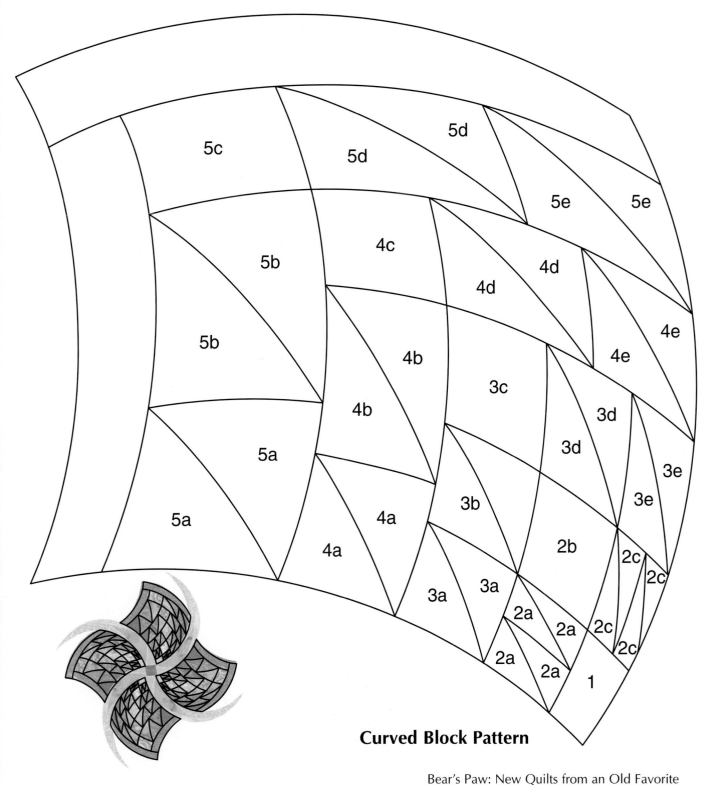

Curved Block Pattern

2nd Place

A Night to Remember

50" x 66". Photo by Rick Holt and Jerry Carrell.

Bear's Paw: New Quilts from an Old Favorite

Photo by Rick Holt and Jerry Carrell

Gayle Wallace   Gertrude Embree

The two "bear stars" retain their individuality and create a third form where they partially merge.

Meet the quilters

Gertrude: Gayle and I began collaborating in 1995 for the MAQS Ohio Star competition. We usually work individually; however, Gayle likes the challenge of working on my unconventional designs, and I like her expertise and willingness to risk going into new territory with her quilting. We have had three quilts accepted for these MAQS competitions, which require us to use a traditional block in a new way.

Working together has been an interesting journey. One path we've followed has led us into the world of modern technology. Like many quiltmakers, we both enjoy the slow meditative processes of hand sewing, but we have more ideas than time. The new methods of rotary cutting, quick piecing, and machine quilting speed the process and make it possible to explore a series of ideas like our Bear's Paw quilts. The computer helps us both to exchange news, plans, and schedules via e-mail. I especially like using the computer as a design tool, while Gayle uses it to organize paperwork for her classes. Her scanner and new digital camera allow her to send me pictures of work in progress. In the winter, we live an hour apart, but in the summer and fall, I am 1,500 miles from Louisiana.

When I finish the designing and sewing of the quilt top, we meet for a day in Gayle's studio. A remodeled trailer houses her long-arm quilting machine, design wall, and office. Seven years of experience and hundreds of quilts have honed her skills on that formidable machine. We push each other during this session. I have a vision for the quilting design, and she offers alternate suggestions. Her experience helps to predict pitfalls to avoid, although ripping out is an option we have both endured. Eventually, an agreement is reached, and the work is completed. She is elated. I am doubtful.

17

Inspiration and design

I began playing with the Bear's Paw on the computer. With a draw-and-paint computer program, I was able to copy the block and move the copy anywhere in relation to the original. The block background was left transparent, which produced secondary patterns. I created a series of these interlocked Bear's Paw designs. When long "claws" were added to big paws, the result was a star pattern. I chose the most interesting for the first quilt in our Bear's Paw series. The scale was enlarged, new elements were added to the centers of the blocks, and THE FOUR BEARS, a new constellation, was born.

For our second quilt, I experimented with an overlapping set. The blocks do not meet edge to edge, but the design lines overlap and create a new form in the merger. The simplest of these overlapping paw designs became the basis for A NIGHT TO REMEMBER. The design of the background was added later, after the central image had been transferred to graph paper for a working plan. The background was planned to suggest an explosion of light, perhaps an event in the sky, perhaps an interior event. Value changes in the background colors served to create a frame without the addition of a border.

18

Where the colors of the two blocks merged, a third color was created. Many scraps were dye painted to produce this effect. The binding and some of the background fabrics were dyed to achieve the correct values. The idea that the quilting would be a featured element of the work influenced decisions from the initial design stage to the color, value, and fabric decisions.

Both of us thought the quilting should neither overpower the design of the top nor be obscured by it. Gayle was willing to put aside all her traditional stencils and work out strategies to cover the quilt's surface with lush stitching and original patterns. She enjoys using colored quilting threads and changed the thread color many times when the design required it. I had the pleasure of adding the final bits of embroidery and beading. It was a delight to embellish the beautiful quilted surface.

Gayle: The part I enjoy the most is creating the quilting designs. For such elaborate quilting, we placed a clear plastic sheet over the top of the quilt for doodling. With the use of dry-erase pens, quilting possibilities can be created but just as easily erased when something doesn't work.

When Gertrude gives me her graph sheet with the quilting ideas, it's difficult to visualize them full size. Sometimes, the designs look wonderful on paper, but when they are blown up to size, they aren't as effective. We spend a good deal of time creating the quilting designs to be original and inspiring. The leaves in the four corners are done in trapunto with a number of different designs in each of the small squares in the center of the quilt. It took three days to mark and create the original stencils to use on the quilt.

A Night to Remember
details

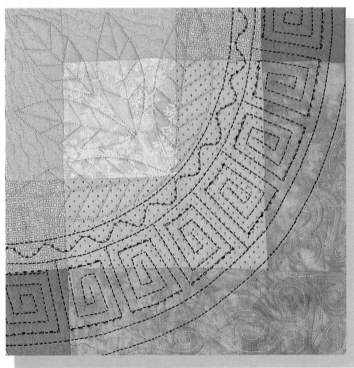

Vanishing

66" x 52"

Bear's Paw: New Quilts from an Old Favorite

Is the bear vanishing behind the blocks, along with our loss of wilderness, or are the blocks, which represent traditional values in quilting and our lives, vanishing?

Meet the quilter

I started quilting by making a family-tree quilt for my grandmother. It included embroidered names of children, grandchildren, and great-grandchildren, but I didn't have any clue about quilting the top, so it was tied.

My husband and I were raised on farms, and after several years, we were able to purchase a farm of our own. It included a 100-year-old home, which needed a lot of remodeling. After an extra bedroom was almost completed, I decided an old iron bed we had purchased at an auction needed a quilt. Still not knowing anything about quilting, I made my second quilt, which was quilted in sections without a frame. I used doubled thread and a very large sharps needle to be sure to get through all the layers. Now, years later, I look back at all my improvements in tools and techniques. The house remodeling is still going on, and hopefully, my growth in quilting is going on too.

Vanishing was inspired by a trip to Alaska we took with my husband's twin brother and his wife. Even though the wilderness is still everywhere you look, it is apparent that civilization is making big changes in our world, even in Alaska.

Inspiration and design

When the quilt was first designed, I wanted the bear to disappear among the Bear's Paw blocks. I first drew a bear with a fish in its mouth, then drafted the blocks on point, with ¼" squares representing 1". With the aid of a light box, the bear was drawn over the blocks. The drawing was then taken to a photocopy shop and enlarged 400 percent so that the ¼" squares were 1". I made two of these enlargements. Both copies were fitted together and spray-glued to poster boards. One was hung so the finished blocks could be pinned to it to check for color intensity. The other copy was used to make templates, which weren't cut apart until I was ready to start a particular block.

21

I didn't always stay with the true block. Some of the sashings were included in the piecing of the block. I wanted the actual shaping of the Bear's Paw tracks repeated in the border and wanted them to be vanishing too. To get this effect, dishwashing gel was used on the border fabric. This product contains bleach, and it is thick, so it doesn't run. I experimented with timing the gel and determined that 15 minutes lightened the fabric as much as needed. I made a stencil of the bear's tracks and drew it on the borders, then put the gel on the fabric. After 15 minutes, I washed all the gel out with clear water and put the fabric in vinegar to neutralize any remaining bleach. The borders were then washed in soapy water and rinsed. Some of the border fabric was bleached to match the the tracks then appliquéd to the quilt body.

I used cotton batting because it seems to grip the quilt top and backing. To hold everything in place, the quilting was done in the ditch in the Bear's Paw blocks that were not in contact with the bear. The rest was quilted freehand, with rayon thread on the top to add just a little light reflection.

Original drawing.

Bear's Paw: New Quilts from an Old Favorite

Bear's Paw: New Quilts from an Old Favorite

Pointed Paws

81" x 92"

Bear's Paw: New Quilts from an Old Favorite

D rafting the basic pattern in a diamond shape transformed the graphics and allowed for more possibilities in arrangement and movement.

Mary Ann Herndon Houston, TX

My Quilting

I started quilting after attending a lecture that Yvonne Porcella gave to my quilt guild in Houston, Texas, many years ago. I had always done some kind of needlework, but since that time, my focus has been on quilting. Like most quilters, I find ideas for new projects in many ways. An advertisement can trigger a color scheme; an illustration in a children's book can initiate a whole thought process. Other forms of art, such as sculpture and paintings, all have an impact on my design process. My husband and I have traveled a lot, and the art and scenery in France and Italy have influenced my color choices to a great extent.

When people ask me why I spend so much time quilting, I tell them it's a fascination with fabric, color, and design. Making a quilt is like creating a painting to me, and the quilts and art pieces that I admire the most are the ones that appear as whole designs at first glance and then lead you to explore the pieces that make up the whole.

Choosing my next project is always frustrating because I have too many ideas to ever complete in my lifetime. I do like competitions, so that will probably guide my next project choice.

Inspiration and design

The annual MAQS contest focusing on creating new quilts from an old favorite always inspires me because it calls for modern approaches to connecting the old with the new. I work a lot with hand-dyed fabrics and especially like the ones that shade from color to color across the fabric. They offer a much more exciting color flow than those having only one gradated color. Pairing a bright-lemon to deep-rust gradation with a wavy ecru and black stripe and a black and gold background gave rise to a seemingly complicated design that was really fairly simple. Deciding on the color placement of the diamonds was a decision made after most of the diamonds had been completed and placed on my design wall.

25

Bear's Paw: New Quilts from an Old Favorite

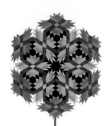

Initially, I planned to graduate from yellow to rust but found the final arrangement emphasized a central bright yellow star.

To start the quilt, I drafted the Bear's Paw as a diamond and made black and white copies of it in a reduced size. Arranging these small diamonds on a design board and standing back to assess the impact helped me choose a setting. After that, I drew several colored tracings over the selected setting and made most of the color decisions. Changing my mind about color placement midway into the process caused me to make more diamonds than I needed, but the result made that time well spent.

I paired bias strips of the background and paw fabrics, sewed the pairs together, and cut the diamonds from the sewn strips. Less fabric was wasted, and the two-color paws were completed and ready to add to the block. The rest of the construction was the same as for a regular Bear's Paw. I sewed each of the four components of each block and then joined those parts

with the intersecting wavy striped rectangles to form the diamond.

After the diamonds were sewn together, I had to tackle the decision as to what to do with the four corners, which is always problematic when placing blocks on point. But, in this case, the black and gold background fabric seemed the obvious choice because it allowed the wavy stripes to continue into the border. The same diamond shape was used, but the black fabric was substituted for the block.

The decision to use diagonal stripes in the border was made after all the rest of the quilt had been completed. The irregular, rather irreverent striping formed a vibrant contrast to the black corners and connected the border to the interior colors.

If my machine quilting was better, I would have machine quilted this piece because the hand quilting was endless. It still needed more when I sent it in to the contest. The quilting in the diamonds was an integral part of the design, so the time was worth it.

26

10" 60° Diamond Block

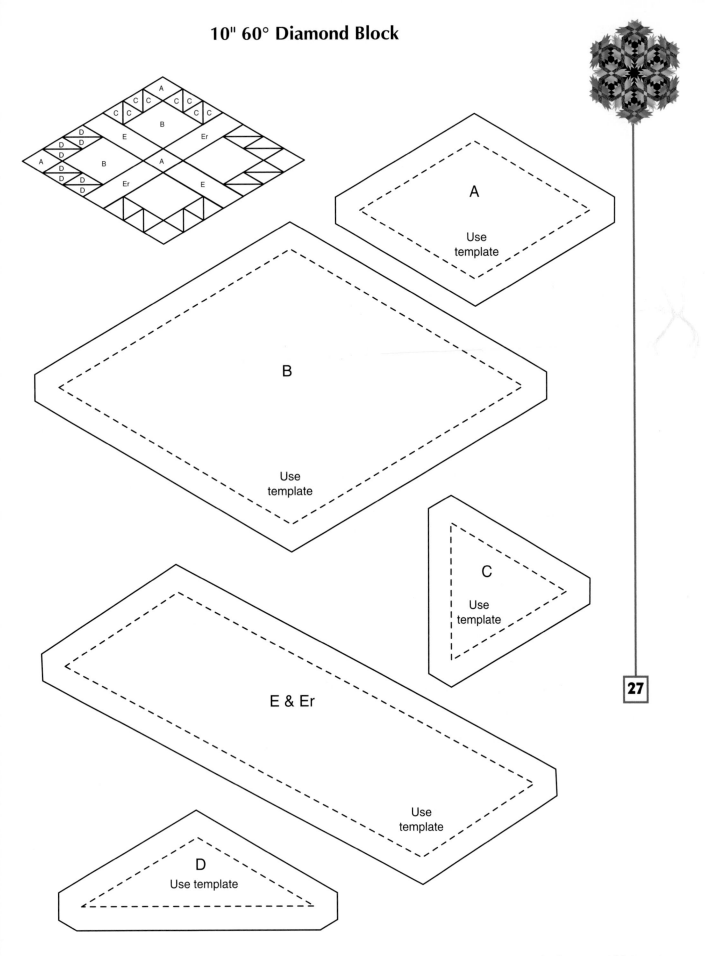

A

Use template

B

Use template

C

Use template

E & Er

Use template

D
Use template

Last Breath of Spring – Greenwood Ridge

66" x 55"

Bear's Paw: New Quilts from an Old Favorite

Laura Fogg Ukiah, CA

T he outer pieced border was chosen because there are still bears in these hills. I've seen their paw prints.

Meet the Quilter

I am a relatively new quilter, having joined a quilt group just three years ago. I didn't really get hooked, though, until three things happened almost simultaneously, a quilt group series project, a two-week rafting trip through the Grand Canyon, and a collage quiltmaking class. I suddenly found myself practically obsessed with creating a Grand Canyon collage series, followed immediately by a Mendocino County fence-line series. Now, quilt inspirations are everywhere, and I regret only the lack of time to realize them all.

Quilting hit me as the answer to a lifelong search for the right medium. I've always been an artist but never felt completely sure of myself with ink, paint, or clay. With fabric and thread, I have no doubts. Images come into my mind that I can create instantly. My goal in all of my art, and now especially in my quilts, is to show people how I see the beautiful world around me. My world is not static or ordered. It is full of movement and energy. Even on a windless day, the plants are growing and the air is vibrating as the sun heats it. Landscapes of solid rock are alive with lines that compel me to enter and discover where water used to flow. Life is radiant in all its forms, and it is an incredibly positive experience for me to be able to share my vision. There are a hundred ideas in my head for every quilt that I actually make.

For my next project, I am looking forward to doing a commission for Fetzer Winery, to create a quilt commemorating a family-owned cherry farm, which was a special part of our community for generations. The cherry farm is gone now, but I want to help people remember how much they loved the place and the people who ran it.

Inspiration and design

LAST BREATH OF SPRING – GREENWOOD RIDGE is a collage quilt, a collage of fabrics and techniques. It represents the many layers of my emotional connection with this beautiful county where I have lived and worked for 30 years. It is part of a series of quilts depicting the

29

old, broken-down fence lines that I see while driving to work on the lonely roads between the inland valleys and the coast.

The center landscape panel was inspired by a couple of photos taken on the ridge, but I relied primarily on my memory of how it had felt to stand there in the clean, warm air with everything around me moving in the breeze.

Collage landscape construction

The center collage panel was made without any patterns or preliminary drawings. It was truly a create-as-you-go project. It was made in distinct stages, working from back to front, with the foreground details saved for last.

I arbitrarily decided how big to make the panel, cut a rectangular piece of backing fabric that size, and put it on my work table, face down. Over the backing, I placed a piece of cotton batting, which became my blank canvas. Then, working from the sky in the most distant background to the more detailed weeds and grasses in the foreground, I free-hand cut, layered, and wove raw-edged strips and pieces of dozens of fabrics into a collage. I worked fast to capture the energy.

All of the fabrics were commercial cottons in geometric or abstract prints. I never use sky prints, tree prints, or florals because it is not possible for me to achieve any depth or movement with somebody else's conception of these landscape elements. To me, the light playing on the clouds or the distant hills is alive and different in every part of the composition, and I just add, move, and change fabrics until it feels right. At this stage, nothing is pinned or sewn, so it's easy to be flexible. I did not concern myself with intricate detail, because the landscape was planned to be

the background for the wildflower appliqués, which were added later.

Once the landscape panel made me happy, I cut a piece of tulle the right size and carefully positioned it over the whole thing. I chose a dark purple tulle, which was almost invisible over the sky and hills but which accentuated the purples of the brodiaea flowers in the meadow. Unless I'm looking for a misty effect, I generally use a dark-colored tulle because pale colors reflect too much light and wash out the composition. Working from the center toward the edges, I carefully smoothed and pinned the tulle to the rest of the layers in the center panel. I used long, slender straight pins because they don't push the carefully layered fabrics around as much as safety pins would, but it is necessary to work carefully when quilting to avoid getting poked. Using all kinds of variegated rayon thread, I machine quilted the panel freehand, without marks or any pre-conceived notion of where I was going, so it felt a bit like drawing with pen and ink.

In the last stage, the foreground brodiaea flowers and leaves were superimposed over the whole composition. Again, to capture the lightness and movement of wild living things, I used raw-edge appliqué with energetic, unplanned machine stitching. Nothing was pinned this time. I let the fabric move and bunch under the feed dogs of my machine and literally went with the flow.

I like to incorporate traditional patterns into my quilts as a means of reminding myself what quilting is all about. Maybe the person who strung this fence so many years ago came home to a cabin in which he stayed warm on a cold night under a hand-pieced quilt.

30

LAST BREATH OF SPRING –
GREENWOOD RIDGE
details

The Bear and the Boy:
I Spy the Disappearing Bear's Paw

74" x 74"

Bear's Paw: New Quilts from an Old Favorite

There are 22 full and partial Bear's Paw blocks in the body of the quilt.

Meet the quilter

Fabric and sewing have been a part of my life for 38 years, ever since fourth grade 4H. But eight years ago, when I took my first quilting class, a whole new world of artistic expression opened for me. The art of quiltmaking is now my passion.

My quilts fluctuate between traditional with a twist and contemporary art quilts. I love to use bold colors, unusual fabrics, and a combination of unconventional techniques. My quilt designs are original, and I challenge myself to use many fabrics in one project and not limit myself to any one technique. The quilts are pieced and quilted by machine, and they often include various embellishments, such as bobbin work or machine free-motion thread painting.

I enjoy passing on my passion for quilting by teaching classes from my home and creating quilting projects for students at my children's schools. I also enjoy opportunities to lecture to local groups about the art of quiltmaking, including a trunk show of examples. Several of my quilts have been accepted in International Quilt Association and American Quilter's Society shows and displayed in local galleries and our local library.

When not planning a new quilting project, preparing for a class, or stitching, I am the car-pool queen for my three children, ages 10, 12, and 17; a volunteer for their activities; and a companion to my very supportive spouse.

Inspiration and design

My first visit to the Museum of the American Quilter's Society was in April 2000. I spent hours enjoying the museum, including the Storm at Sea exhibition. That experience moti-vated me to create this Bear's Paw quilt.

My initial design was inspired by my 12-year-old son and his stuffed Kodiak bear. I imag-ined the bear nearly full size. The image of the boy and the bear sitting next to each other

came to me in the middle of the night, then I began to picture bordering the quilt in traditionally pieced Bear's Paw blocks.

The story of the quilt slowly emerged over time. The bear is crying because his habitat is being destroyed by the clear cutting of trees, the building of highways, and the polluting of cities. The boy represents future generations and the hope that, with compassion, they can help stop the destruction of our natural lands.

My original sketch was enlarged to the full size of the quilt (Figure 1). Then I made freezer-paper templates of each pattern piece to create the curved pieced background. The bear and the boy are machine appliquéd, and the city is fused to the background. The pine tree was created with free-motion bobbin work. Nearly 100 different fabrics were used in the quilt.

The "I Spy" camouflaged blocks came to me as the quilt was being constructed (Figure 2). The pieces of the hidden blocks were held in place with glue stick, then raw-edged appliquéd by machine. It was fun choosing fabrics that blended rather than contrasted with each other. Finally, while preparing slides for the contest, I realized several of the blocks needed to be couched with yarn so they could be seen by the camera's eye.

Selecting fabrics

As quilters, we have so many wonderful resources for fabrics, and the colors available are all so yummy, that we are often frozen in our tracks trying to choose. To select colors for my quilt, I decided to use a color wheel (page 37), the mention of which may invite you to reminisce about your fourth-grade art class or cause you to doze off. But, now, as you pursue making your wonderful quilts, the color wheel could become your newest best friend.

I invite you to play with the color wheel to learn how it can help you select a color strategy to use as a spring board for your next project. It's also a good idea to spend time learning the concepts of value (light, medium, and dark) and contrast (amount of difference) and how important they can be in your quilt designs.

34

Fig. 1. *Original sketch.*

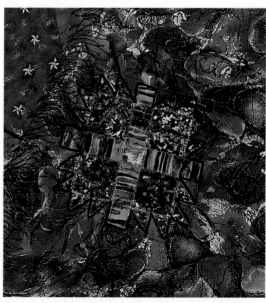

Fig. 2. *Close-up of a hidden block in the bear.*

Bear's Paw: New Quilts from an Old Favorite

Take time to play with your stash and arrange your fabrics by color family and by lights, mediums, and darks within each family. Through this process, you will see, by the sizes of the piles, which color families you tend to choose most often. You will also discover which colors and values are overstocked or missing altogether.

When sorting your fabrics by value, do not worry initially about the print or design of the fabric. You might have a medium-value large plaid next to a medium-value medium-sized floral, next to a medium-value tone-on-tone. The print of the fabric is less important than its value when combined with other fabrics.

Here's how I used these color principles in planning and executing THE BEAR AND THE BOY. I wanted to use earth tones and greens. Referring to my original sketch, I chose a fabric from my stash for the bear's body. It had shades of burnt red and orange as well as browns and black. On the color wheel, green and orange and purple form a triad, that is, three colors spaced equi distant from each other on the wheel. These three colors became the primarly colors for the quilt. I used several different greens to represent the forested areas, browns to oranges for earth tones, and purples for my mountains (Figure 3).

Just to confirm my choices, I placed tracing paper over my sketch and used colored pencils to see how all the colors worked together (Figure 4, page 36). This step helped me to see potential problems, such as needing to use a darker value in one spot or a lighter value in another.

Once the main colors had been chosen, I began pulling fabric from my stash that belonged in those color families. The next thing to consider was the value of each color. Because the fabric for the bear's body was a wonderfully mottled medium-dark value, all the fabrics that touched the body needed to have enough contrast to stand out. To be certain there was enough contrast, I pinned the fabrics on a design wall and stood back to view the color choices from a distance.

Fig. 3. *Detail of the mountains, showing how a variety of fabrics of similar value in the same color family can be used together.*

I chose medium to medium-light greens for the forest around the bear. The boy's shirt needed to be a medium-light value of orange to stand out as well. The deep purple mountain top was darker in value, so it appeared farther away, and the lavender mountain was lighter in value to show it was closer. I had to audition all of the purples to be sure they contrasted enough with the bear. For the city background, the sky needed to look smoggy, but it could not be so dark that the buildings would not stand out. Choosing these fabrics took several attempts.

Choosing fabrics for the bear's nose was difficult too. Several creamy white fabrics did not have enough contrast. Finally, I chose a very white fabric but still had to stitch around the nose with a heavy black thread in the bobbin to help the nose stand out clearly enough.

Overall, I was very pleased with how all of the design elements came together. Past attempts and outcomes from other projects have demonstrated to me several key elements. First, it is important to take the time to see how each fabric relates to the others by color and value. Second, it helps to stop often and stand back to confirm that the fabric choices are working the way they were envisioned, and third, be sure to savor the creative process.

Fig. 4. *Colored-pencil version.*

THE BEAR AND THE BOY detail.

Bear's Paw: New Quilts from an Old Favorite

Color Wheel

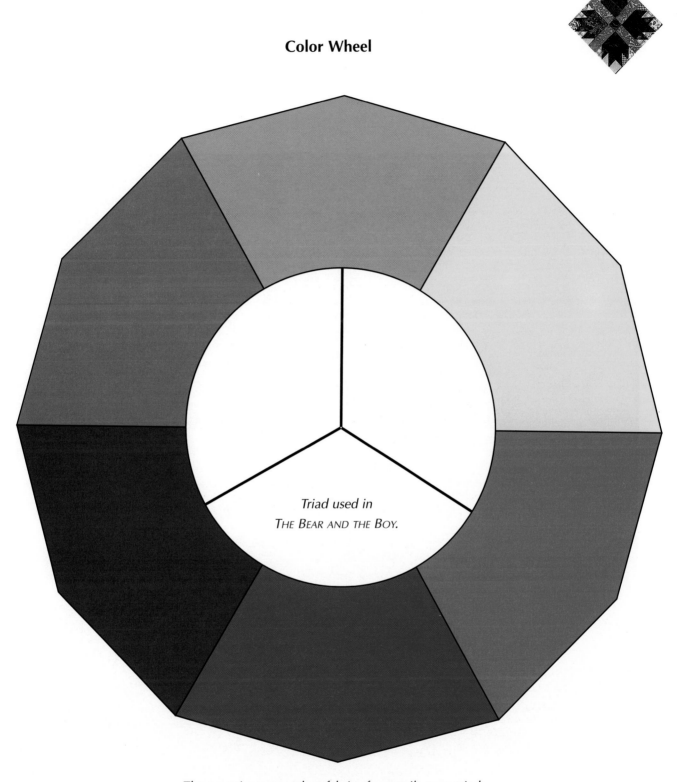

Triad used in
THE BEAR AND THE BOY.

The next time you select fabrics for a quilt, try a triad;
that is, any three colors equidistant from each other on the color wheel.

Buggy Wheels

55" x 55"

Bear's Paw: New Quilts from an Old Favorite

I had envisioned something entirely different, but this quilt seemed to have a mind of its own.

Meet the quilter

I began quilting in 1984 when a box of fabric and a pattern showed up on my doorstep from my mother-in-law, Ruth Clem. She thought that I needed a hobby because I had quit working to raise our two sons. She also remembered that I had stopped to admire a quilt in a show-room window on one of our shopping sprees. Until that time, I had never seen a quilt.

My mother had taught/fought me to sew clothing, and in hindsight, I am very grateful for her persistence. With that sewing background, learning to make quilts came quickly. My first quilt was a Log Cabin. Well, first quilts are always first quilts, but it received such rave reviews from the family that quilting just stuck. I made another…and another….

Then I met a quilter who became a good friend, Linda Deutsch. One of her first comments to me was, "Barb, you make the most beautiful quilt tops, why would you ruin them with your 'crunky' machine quilting?" In looking at my quilts, I had already seen that I was lacking something and that my friend's hand quilting really added that extra spark to hers. I decided to take the time to learn to hand quilt.

Competing in quilt shows was just second nature. With this step, I was fortunate to know an accomplished, award-winning quilter, Lois K. Ide. It was through her, that my quilts started taking on new direction. Looking back through all those quilts and all those years, it is total-ly amazing to me how much I have grown. Each time I felt there was a plateau, I grew past it, first in technical skills and then in design. There is so much to learn. Quilting is an art and I love it.

Inspiration and design

The idea for BUGGY WHEELS began when I created a quilt for a special exhibit with the theme Nine Patch Divided. I used only 100-percent cotton fabrics. The hand-dyed colors seemed to lend themselves well to the sage-green, commercially dyed background, thus creating a

unique color palette. In addition, the values and solid colors were chosen to show the hand-quilting stitches.

After a few blocks had been machine pieced, the central star became apparent, not a strong star, but a star nonetheless. The lavender strip insets were added because additional color was needed, thus creating the wheel effect. The challenge was to set the blocks and balance the design without losing the star. The larger deep-purple triangles finished off the piecing beautifully, adding variety and framing the design. Having created the wheels in this Amish-like piece, I chose straight-line quilting for continuity.

Remarkably, the quilt also contains the Bear's Paw blocks, making it eligible for the MAQS contest in addition to the Nine Patch Divided exhibit. It was really exciting to create a timeless rather than trendy piece.

Buggy Wheels has been juried into several other prestigious shows, including the 2000 AQS show, and the 1999 International Quilt Association show in Houston, Texas. It also won first place in the Invitational Category of the 1999 Kaleidoscope of Quilts Show in Toledo, Ohio, and it received the John Flynn Faculty Choice Award at the 2000 Minnesota Quilter's Conference Show in Minneapolis.

40

Selecting fabrics

One of the most widely made remarks about my quilt has been, "What a gorgeous color palette." Because this quilt didn't turn out the way I had envisioned it, perhaps you would like to know how the color scheme was derived.

Many people use the color wheel. I use instinct. As a quilter, you learn over the years that you have certain preferences – some people prefer appliqué vs. piecing...cotton batting vs. polyester batting...machine quilting vs. hand quilting. Initially, I had envisioned a gradated palette for this quilt, but it was not meant to be. The bright hand-dyed fabrics with the look of solid colors intrigued me, so that was what I chose to use. The solids would have blended well with any type of background fabric, be it floral, print, or solid, but I wanted my hand quilting to show. That requirement ruled out florals and prints, so a solid color was selected for the background.

This is where value came into play. Value is the relative lightness or darkness of a color. The quilting stitches would not have shown on dark values, so I looked for light to medium values in the solid colors. Off I went to the fabric store with most of my hand-dyed fabrics. I pulled out bolt after bolt and fanned them out to find which color I liked. My choices were unlimited, but the sage green was lovely with the hand-dyed fabrics. A design wall proved to be a valuable asset when viewing the quilt in progress. I consulted it frequently.

You can use these simple color strategies in your quilts, too. If you would like to experiment, you can audition different fabrics on a design wall and see how they change your design. Play with the fabrics until you like what you see, but most of all, enjoy yourself!

13½" Bear's Paw with Nine Patch Block

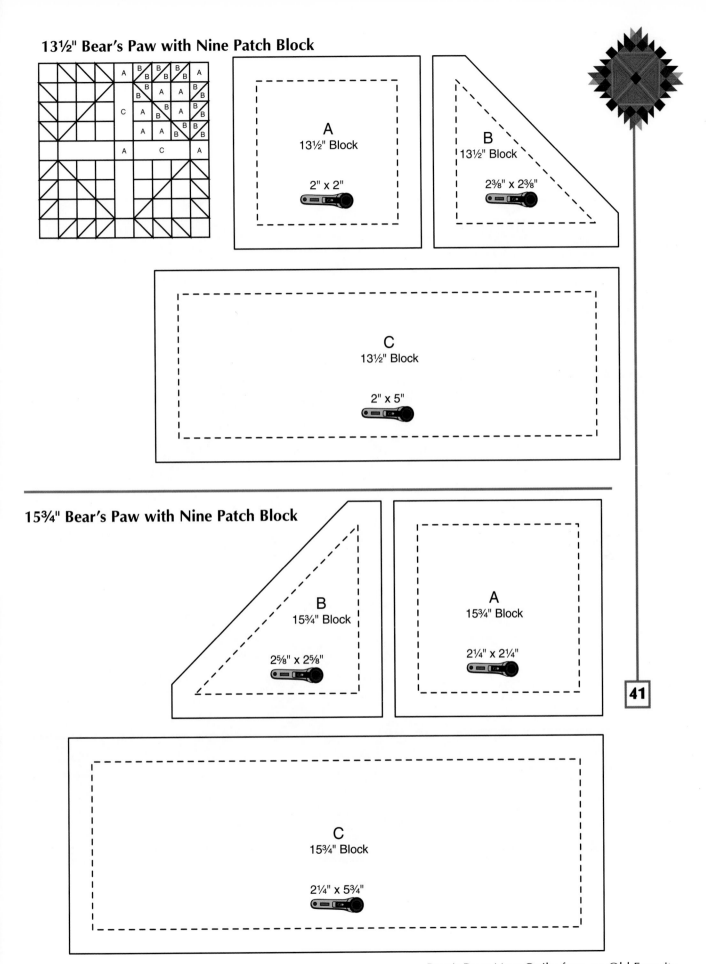

A
13½" Block

2" x 2"

B
13½" Block

2⅜" x 2⅜"

C
13½" Block

2" x 5"

15¾" Bear's Paw with Nine Patch Block

B
15¾" Block

2⅝" x 2⅝"

A
15¾" Block

2¼" x 2¼"

C
15¾" Block

2¼" x 5¾"

41

Sammamish

52" x 52"

Bear's Paw: New Quilts from an Old Favorite

I named this quilt for my city, which lies on the east side of Lake Sammamish in my home state of Washington.

Meet the quilter

Ten years ago, while on a lunch break from my job as a software engineer, I found my way into a small quilt shop. I poked around in the fabric for a little while until a pattern caught my eye. It was very geometric and appealed to the mathematician in me. After purchasing the pattern and selecting four different fabrics, I began working on my first quilt, without having a clue about ¼" seams, rotary cutting, and the like.

Part of the quilt is hand pieced and part is machine pieced. It has the fluffiest batting possible, and it is hand quilted, which took me four years to complete. A marvel of poor craftsmanship, it is nevertheless one of my favorites because it opened the world of quilting to me.

Since that time, I have taken quilting and design classes and filled my sewing room with gadgets. My technique has improved significantly, and using only four different fabrics in a quilt is unthinkable. Rather, I find myself hand dyeing fabrics to get that perfect shade and spending hours in fabric shops, eyeing the latest designs and purring over the feel of fine cotton sateen.

When working on one quilt, I usually have three to four others in my mind just waiting for me to translate them into fabric. All types of quilts appeal to me, from a simple baby quilt that takes a weekend, to the more complex art quilt that haunts me night and day for months on end. When they are finished, however, I love them all equally.

Inspiration and design

The Bear's Paw is my favorite traditional pattern. I have made many Bear's Paw quilts and have used this traditional design in the same way, always the same light versus dark proportions and always in a traditional grid pattern. The MAQS contest provided an exciting opportunity to change my approach, and with the encouragement of my quilting buddy,

Tamara Williams, I decided to try to design a Bear's Paw quilt. I wanted to create a sense of paws within paws. After a lot of sketching, erasing, and redrawing, I came up with a possible design. Sketching in black and white allowed me to see the overall structure of the quilt without being influenced by color and texture (Figure 1).

In choosing fabrics, I thought of an English garden and went looking for florals and greens. However, some bold fabrics caught my eye, and I decided to go with my instincts.

The most difficult part of creating this quilt was piecing the spiky inner border. I used a template from a Mariner's Compass pattern for the design (Figure 2). If I were to use this pattern again, I would try to foundation piece the border. After the top was finished, the quilt had a Native American feel, so I decided to use petroglyphs in the quilting design. This aspect of the design also influenced the naming of this quilt.

Fig. 1. *Original sketch.*

Fig. 2. *A Mariner's Compass star point was used to make the border.*

10½" Paw Within a Paw Block

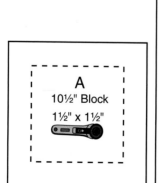

A
10½" Block
1½" x 1½"

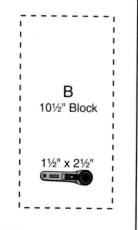

B
10½" Block

1½" x 2½"

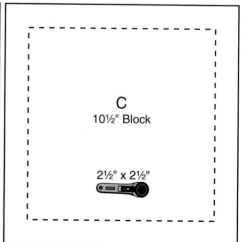

C
10½" Block

2½" x 2½"

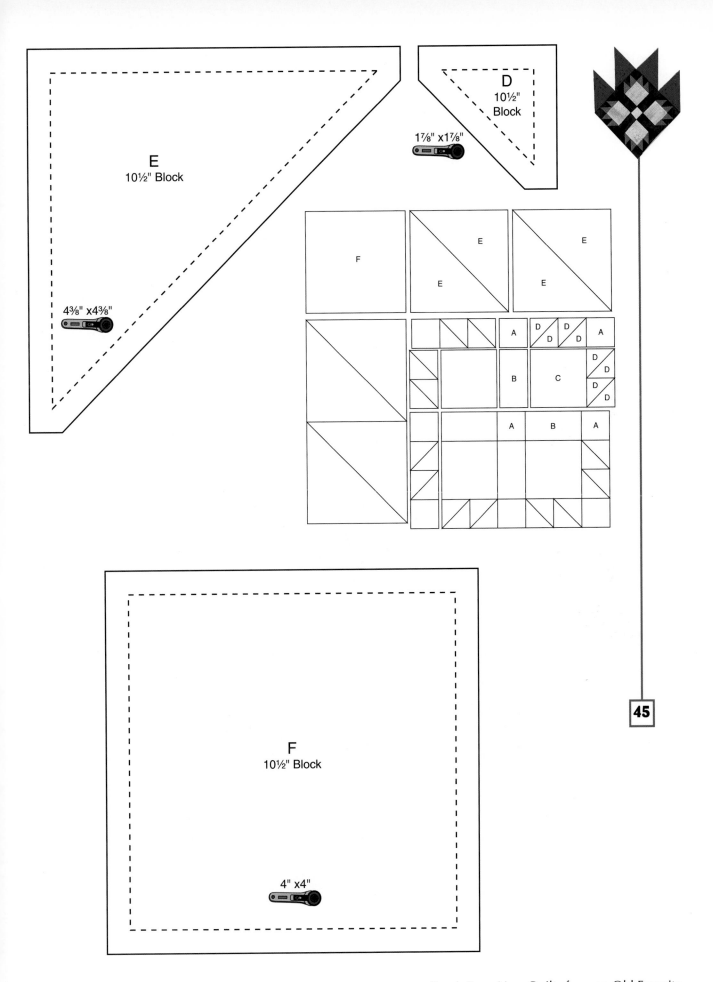

E
10½" Block

4⅜" x4⅜"

D
10½" Block

1⅞" x1⅞"

F

E

E

E

E

A   D   D   A
     D   D

B   C   D
          D
          D
          D

A   B   A

F
10½" Block

4" x4"

Bear's Paw: New Quilts from an Old Favorite

45

Golden Blocks and the Three Bears

62" x 62"

Bear's Paw: New Quilts from an Old Favorite

*P*utting Mama, Papa, and Baby
bear in the same block was
no trouble at all.

Meet the quilter

Music was my first love. I was the music director of my church and taught elementary music
in the public school system. I also taught private piano in my home and at the local junior
college. When I retired and these jobs came to an end in 1990, I was ready for a new challenge and decided quilting would be it. I had enjoyed sewing for my girls and myself, so
quilts would be great. After all, one size fits all.

Getting involved with other quilters seemed like the proper thing to do, so I attended my first
quilt guild meeting. The show-and-tell segment was tremendous, and there I met wonderfully talented, artistic quiltmakers, happily showing their creations, and beginning quilters
happy with their first attempts. I was so inspired. It was wonderful. I bought a book, checked
out a video on hand piecing from the guild library, took an appliqué class and a hand quilting class at a local quilt shop, and was on my way.

I love color and a lot of it. I think that explains why scrap quilts are so appealing to me.
Putting all those colors together is the most exciting part. Five UFOs (unfinished objects) are
now hanging in my quilt room. Two wedding projects, a class project, a small landscape,
and a border project for the guild. I also have at least six more ideas in my head.

47

I love giving nice gifts, and no one ever complains about receiving a quilt. Each of our seven
granddaughters has a baby quilt, a "napper" quilt, and I have just completed the seventh and
youngest granddaughter's bed quilt. During a chicken-pox siege, we made doll quilts. The
girls did what they could do, and I did the rest. We were all happier for the experience.

Blessed by a supportive husband and family and quilters in general, who continually amaze
me with their aesthetic display of color and design, I shall remain a quilter as long as I can.
What fun!

Inspiration and design

For a long time, I had wanted to make a golden quilt that would reflect the hues that God put in our Southern Illinois autumns. During the year, I had purchased gold print fabric for that project. While viewing Pineapple quilts from a previous MAQS contest, I picked up the available literature about upcoming competitions. With the Bear's Paw block the designated pattern for the 2001 contest, it all seemed to come together for me. A golden Bear's Paw quilt would be the perfect choice. After all, "New Quilts from an Old Favorite" is right down my alley. That's what I do.

To draft the block and make it exactly the right size to show off the fabrics properly, I used a computer program. From my fabric stash, I pulled all the golden print fabrics and arranged them in order, from light to dark, along the back of a couch. From the fabrics on the couch, I began constructing blocks, mixing lights, mediums, and darks appropriately. I placed the blocks on my design wall and tried many settings. When there were problems balancing and blending, I called in my daughter and daughter-in-law. They are both school teachers and are good at objective, constructive criticism. Once the setting was selected, I made some blending blocks for specific places.

After the quilt top was finished, it was put away for a few months. When I got it out again, I really liked it. Polyester batting was used to give a soft, airy feeling to the cotton quilt, and it was easy to hand quilt. A stencil was used for the grapes and leaves. The quilted circles on the Bear's Paw blocks were intended to soften and add movement to the piece. In retrospect, waiting to sew the blocks together until I was pleased with every block would have shortened the construction time. Maybe I'll do that next time. Maybe not.

Design ideas

The finished size of the Three Bears block is a 9" square. You can, of course, draft this block to any size and possibly use several sizes of the block in the same quilt. Any one of numerous settings could be used. Combining traditional Bear's Paw blocks and the Three Bears blocks might be a good idea, or you could use a different color for each of the three bears, Baby, Mama, and Papa. Quilting circles on the toes and pads of the feet would be fun to try.

Here are a few more ideas to get your creative juices flowing: pigeon-toed bears, dancing bears, hibernating bears, polar bears, and don't forget...The Bear Went Over the Mountain. Who knows what those feet could do? Happy pawing!

48

9" Three Bears Block

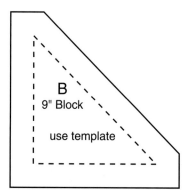

B
9" Block

use template

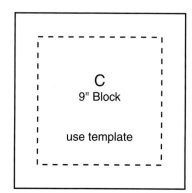

C
9" Block

use template

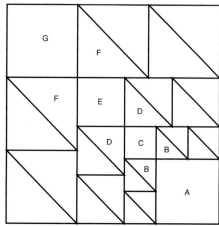

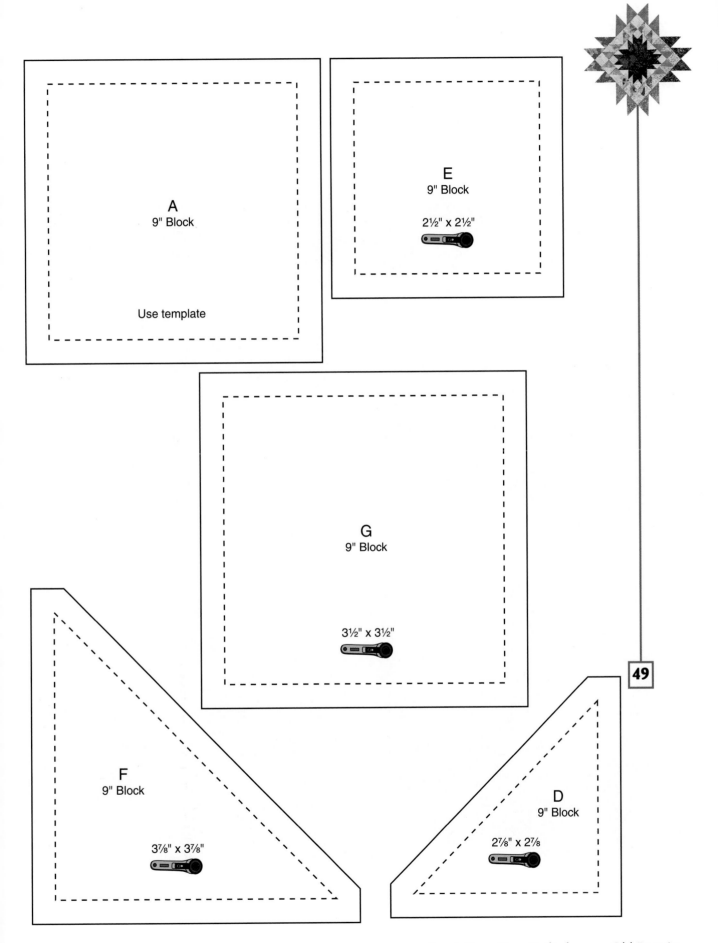

A
9" Block

Use template

E
9" Block

2½" x 2½"

G
9" Block

3½" x 3½"

F
9" Block

3⅞" x 3⅞"

D
9" Block

2⅞" x 2⅞"

49

Lone Bear

56" x 56"

Bear's Paw: New Quilts from an Old Favorite

I n placing the patches on my design wall, I was surprised to see my quilt taking on a Southwestern look.

Meet the quilter

I've always loved fabric. My mother and grandmother loved fabric, too, and let me use their scraps for art and sewing projects. When I was 8 years old, Mom taught me to use her machine, and I've been sewing ever since.

Throughout the years, I've done needlepoint, cross stitch, smocking, and sewn many garments. My passion for quilting blossomed in 1987 after discovering quilt shops, taking a few classes, and joining several quilting groups. I made a few quilts from patterns but soon found tremendous satisfaction in designing my own.

I always have several projects going at the same time – something in the design stage, a top to piece, and another to quilt. I love to enter contests, especially those based on a theme or design challenge. Deadlines push me to finish projects. My love for quiltmaking has provided me with fabulous opportunities to teach, judge, and lecture, and now I edit for a quilting magazine.

Inspiration and design

Each year, I look forward to playing with the traditional block chosen for the MAQS contest. The Bear's Paw has never been a favorite of mine because of the strong "plus" shape in the block's center, but I thought it would be fun to try to transform the block. To begin a medallion design, I drew a single Bear's Paw on point. The addition of a few more lines created a big star. To unify the design, I repeated the claw shapes, moving them out from the center and then connecting them with a zigzag inner border.

Then it was time to see how the design would look in fabric. From my collection of cotton ikats, I picked two multicolored pieces for the block. To help break up the large squares, I cut exact repeats from the fabric with the larger design.

Bear's Paw: New Quilts from an Old Favorite

The central design started with a black background fabric. For weeks, I tried to choose fabrics for the rest of the quilt, but nothing seemed quite right. When stuck, I often ask my husband, Rob, for advice. He suggested changing the background to a dark purple. He was right! The yellows, oranges, and greens glowed in their new setting.

Choosing quilting motifs

Quilting can make the difference between an ordinary quilt and a spectacular one, so the quilting needs to be planned carefully. Every quilt has a theme, mood, or personality, and quilting should enhance these.

LONE BEAR took on an unintentional theme with its Southwestern look. To continue the theme in the quilting, I turned to Native American arts and crafts for inspiration. The idea for the large feathered design came from a pottery vase. Many of the other motifs were borrowed from jewelry, rugs, and baskets.

Here are some tips to help you design your quilting:

• Sketch and doodle, and then keep your good drawings. Your drawing skills will improve, and you will gain confidence for free-motion quilting.

• As a machine quilter, buy every continuous-line design you like, knowing you can change sizes if necessary.

• Use a copy machine to enlarge or reduce your designs to fit blocks and borders. Motifs shouldn't be squished in a space nor should they seem dwarfed.

• When marking borders, begin in the corners and make the design flow gracefully. If you have to adjust motifs to fit the side borders, make small changes in several motifs rather than large changes in just one.

• If the top has all straight lines, quilt curves, and conversely, if the top has curvy lines, add some straight ones.

• Quilt fancy designs on plain fabric where they will show and simple lines on busy prints.

• Use background quilting, such as stippling or crosshatching, to showcase fancy motifs.

• Quilt with consistent density to avoid distorting the finished piece.

LONE BEAR Quilting Motifs

Bear's Paw: New Quilts from an Old Favorite

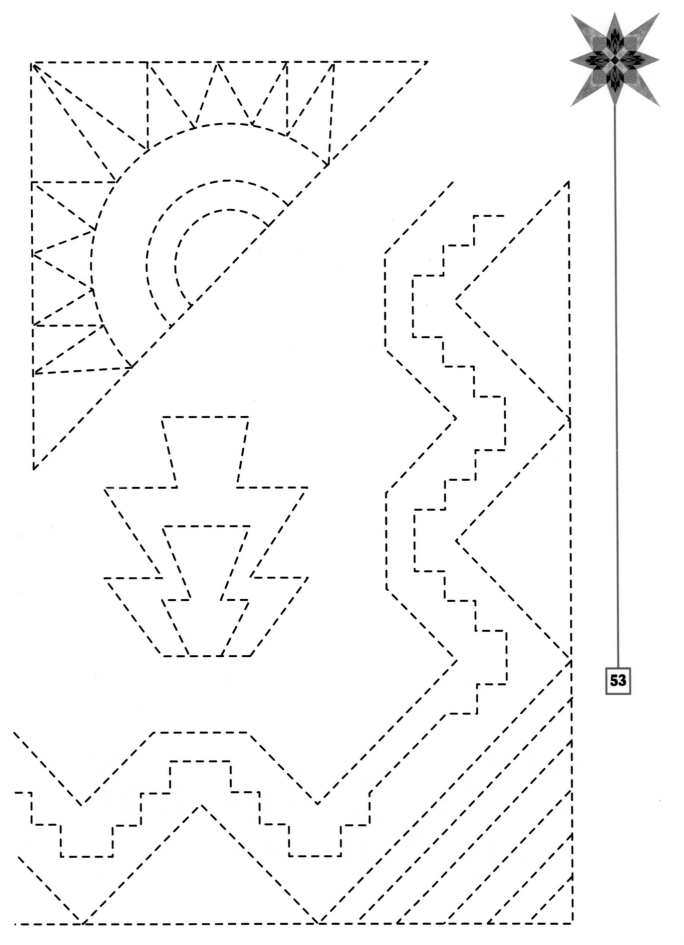

53

Bear's Paw: New Quilts from an Old Favorite

Bears Examination

72" x 72"

Bear's Paw: New Quilts from an Old Favorite

This quilt "bears" examination because the viewer has to look carefully to see how the colors shade from dark to light in different elements of the blocks.

Meet the quilter

I have been sewing since childhood, and my fascination with quilting began when making clothes became boring. I started teaching myself to quilt in 1972 with the help of the only book available to me at the time, *The Standard Book of Quilt Making and Collecting*, by Marguerite Ickis. I have always enjoyed hand piecing but have moved into machine piecing in recent years because there are so many projects to make. I prefer the look and feel of hand quilting and always hand quilt without a frame or hoop of any kind, to be able to move the quilt every which way.

In design, I have been influenced by Jinny Beyer's books and classes. I've made several medallion-style quilts and enjoy working with Jinny's border prints and tone-on-tone fabrics. Otherwise, my quilts are usually some version of a traditional repeated block, with something unusual in the fabrics or the setting. I like to use a limited range of colors, with a wide variety of fabrics and a range of shades, to give the viewer plenty to see.

I love working with fabrics, colors, and design, and enjoy the long-term aspect of quiltmaking, including the processes of designing, choosing fabrics, cutting, piecing, and finally quilting. Finishing a quilt is very rewarding, as is entering quilts in contests. Although I don't often win big, somehow the idea of hundreds of people seeing my quilts is appealing.

My next project is a bed quilt for my best friend of 46 years. It will coordinate with a watercolor painting of irises in her guest bedroom. The fabrics will be in shades of purple, green, and yellow on an off-white background. These are colors I do not often use, so it will be something different for me. I've had to expand my fabric stash considerably…such a pity!

Inspiration and design

This quilt was inspired by a desire to enter the MAQS contest. While I don't make art quilts, the finalists' quilts always include one or two pieces with a repeated traditional block, something I can do.

Bear's Paw: New Quilts from an Old Favorite

I played with the design on paper for quite a while and used colored pencils to try the shading possibilities. I decided that my Bear's Paw quilt would have a limited palette in a wide range of shades, with gradated colors for added interest. The quilt does not have a traditional border because the outer layer of blocks forms the appearance of a border with the reversal of the color arrangement.

Teal, turquoise, rust, and peach have been my favorite colors for a while. I think they make a beautiful complementary combination. I had a pretty good stash of the colors, but to complete the gradations, I had to shop for some very dark and very light fabrics. Like many quilters, I had mostly medium shades.

The fabrics in this quilt are almost all small in scale with no distracting extra colors, because of the strong emphasis on the color gradations. I also included a few larger-scale prints, such as the kangaroo and jungle prints, simply for visual interest.

Multiple half-square triangles

My secret weapon in creating this quilt was a roll of commercial paper for piecing half-square triangles. Without the paper, no matter how carefully I cut the triangles and sewed them together, something seemed to go wrong and they ended up lopsided, with their points either too short or too long.

Commercial papers come in various sizes and are easy to use. Simply cut off the number of units you need from the roll, cut generous rectangles from the two fabrics, place them right sides together, and pin the paper on top. Sew on the dotted lines with a short stitch. Cut the units apart on the solid lines. I keep a rotary cutter just for paper because it does dull the blade. Rip off the paper and press the seam allowances, usually toward the darker side. Voila! You have a perfect square consisting of two half-square triangles. The points match just right with your other pieces. The papers are also available for quarter-square units, which take another step or two but are equally easy to use.

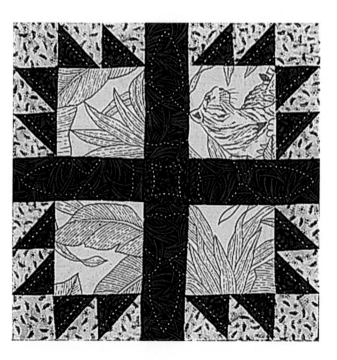

BEAR'S EXAMINATION **detail**

Bear's Paw: New Quilts from an Old Favorite

10" Bear's Paw Block

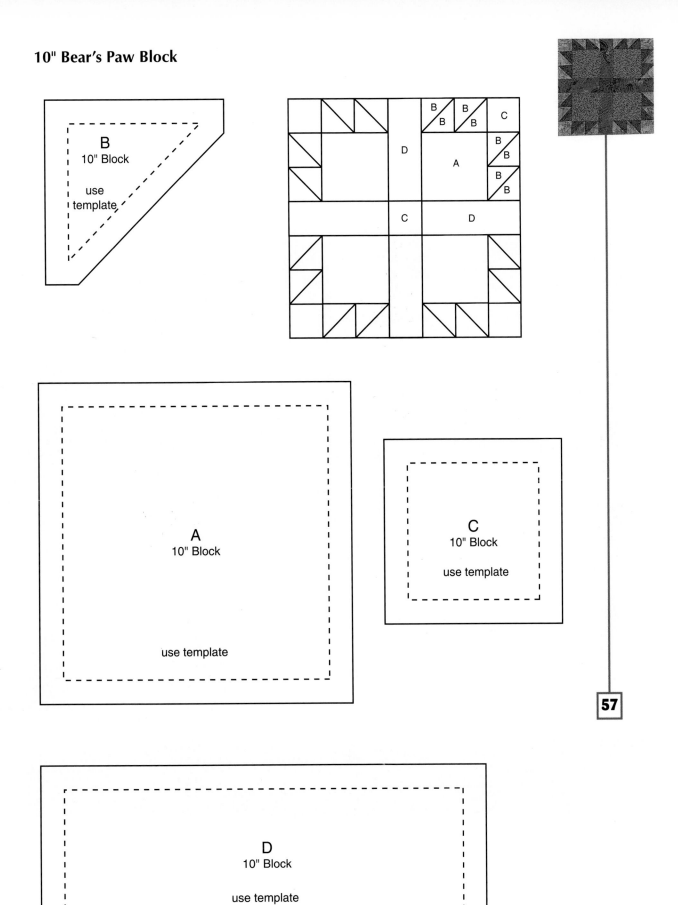

B
10" Block

use template

B B C
B B
D
A
B
B
B
B

C D

57

A
10" Block

use template

C
10" Block

use template

D
10" Block

use template

Bear's Pause

55" x 55"

Bear's Paw: New Quilts from an Old Favorite

Can you find the Mama
and two Baby bears in the
upper-right corner?

Meet the quilter

I had begun sewing as a child and was taking tailoring classes by my senior year of high school. It wasn't until after marriage and children that I discovered quiltmaking. Although I enjoyed my career as a dental hygienist, quilting is like a vacation that can be adjusted to fit the schedules of my husband, Michael, and son, Brad.

I learned to quilt in a class my sister-in-law, Mary Sue Walters, talked me into taking. She never finished her first quilt, but I found my passion. My first teacher, Sharon Grieve, instilled a love for quilting in me and is still a close friend. I began making every pattern available and then started creating techniques and designs when there were no patterns for what was in my head. This was not an easy thing without an art background, but finding I possessed these abilities was a wonderful discovery and truly a blessing. Lately, my work has run more toward the artistic side, with inspiration coming from many talented art quilters. My two favorites would have to be Carol Bryer Fallert and Natalie Sewell.

I began teaching in the early 1990s and love that also. I also love to take challenges and enter competitions. My quilts have won ribbons and been displayed nationally and in Europe. It's very exciting that this is my second quilt to be included in the museum's *New Quilts from an Old Favorite* contest. Entering competitions is such a great way to stir the imagination. I am already envisioning, Tumbling Blocks, the next MAQS contest theme.

Inspiration and design

It started with a workshop on raw-edged landscapes with Natalie Sewell. The class was excellent, but my project didn't please me. Around that same time, I had been thinking about the upcoming MAQS competition. With the thought of combining the class and the competition, an idea struck. I immediately ripped all the trees and foliage off my landscape (they were only put on with glue stick) and began again, this time with a purpose.

A campsite, lake, and sky were added to the background, then the trees and foliage were re-attached. I reasoned that this would be a perfect site for a family of bears to pause. Many paw prints were foundation pieced, and raw-edge reverse appliqué was used to place them around the campfire and even up a tree.

The next question was how to add lawn chairs and the remains of a meal to the scene. I do consulting and product testing for June Tailor, Inc., and had been playing with their new printer fabric, so the idea of taking pictures of these items and printing them on fabric seemed too easy, almost like cheating, but it worked. The rest of the scene was added in raw-edge appliqué.

I wanted to border the quilt with traditional Bear's Paw blocks in some way. I had envisioned a mama and baby bear meandering away in the distance, so these ideas combined in the very subtle effect in the upper-right corner. It was so subtle, in fact, that most people didn't even notice the bears or their tracks through the tall grass until I added one more baby bear in fake fur. The quilt was then sandwiched and free-motion machine quilted to within an inch of its life.

I had so much fun with every step of this quilt, and it truly evolved into something it never started to be. Having the quilt accepted into this prestigious exhibit was truly icing on the cake.

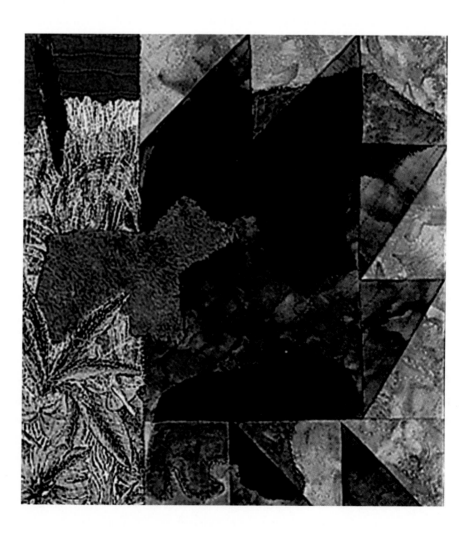

Bear's Paw: New Quilts from an Old Favorite

Bear Appliqué Pattern

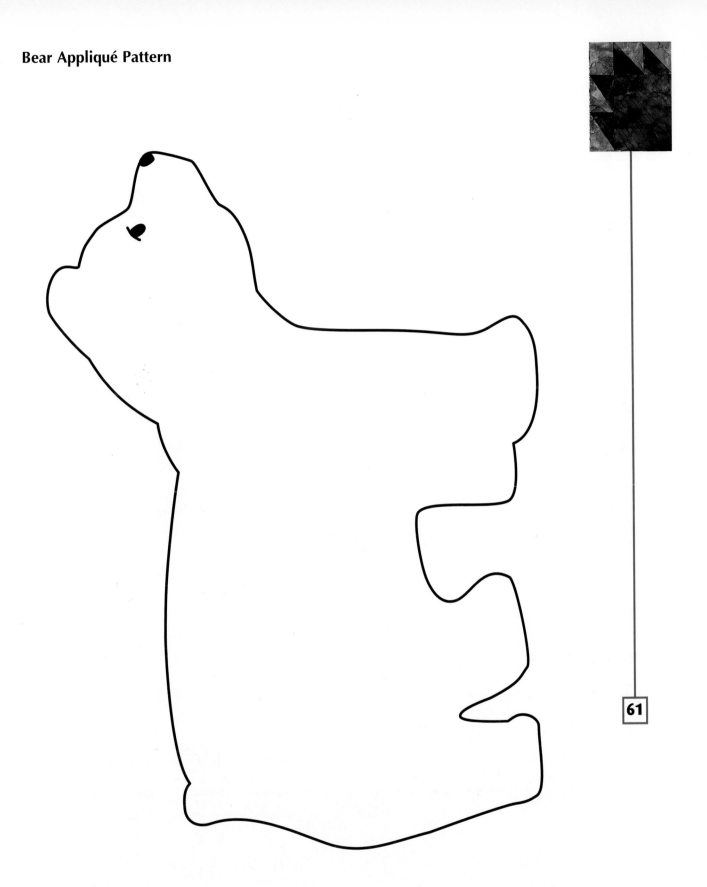

61

Bear Country

64" x 80"

Bear's Paw: New Quilts from an Old Favorite

I wanted my quilt to be divided into four sections, one for each of the four different bears.

Meet the quilter

Starting in high school, I became interested in handwork, including crochet, knitting, crewel embroidery, and appliqué. I made my first appliqué quilt top in 1974, and my grandmother quilted it for me. She had quilted most of her life, as did her mother. Grandma showed me how to quilt, too, but at the time, I could not do it.

Although I did not start to make quilts until after she had passed away in 1983, my grandmother was responsible for instilling the love of quilting in me. I found some quilt patches in her belongings and pieced them together and quilted them in memory of her. I continued quilting by making quilt tops for others, mostly from kits at first. After quilting for more than 17 years now, I usually spend between 10 to 14 hours a day and have made 103 quilts.

God has given me a loving husband who took an interest in my work. He now joins me in quiltmaking. He does a lot of the designing, piecing, and marking. I do the appliqué and the quilting. We make quilts for competition and for customers. We have been fortunate enough to win a lot of contests. For the Bear's Paw quilt, I designed and pieced the top and enjoyed seeing my ideas go from paper to a completed quilt top.

I just finished quilting our next show quilt, and a customer's quilt will be ready to put in the frame soon. Meanwhile, I am tossing ideas around for another contest quilt.

Inspiration and design

There are four sections in the quilt. They are the polar bear, black bear, grizzly, and brown bear. Interlocking Bear's Paws blocks were used to divide my bear countries. A different color was chosen for each section.

First, I sketched my quilt design on graph paper, then broke it down into segments for easier piecing (Figure 1). In the polar and brown bear sections, there is a Bear's Paw block

63

within a larger Bear's Paw block. Some of the toes are elongated in a few of the blocks, and filler blocks were added as needed.

The appliquéd bears in each section are stuffed. I had tried doing this before, without much success. After a stuffed-work class with Anita Shackelford, I was very pleased with the way the bears turned out.

Fig. 1. *Sketch on graph paper. For ease of construction, the quilt was divided into 11 sections, as indicated by the darkened seam lines.*

I could not find all the bears on fabric, so two of the bears are photo transfers.

I was not sure how to finish the quilt and didn't want a pieced border that was too involved. I drew up several border designs and started sewing some together but did not like the way they looked. Finally, I chose the piano-key border. Various fabrics were selected that had already been used in the quilt. The quilting design is different for each section's background. Different colored quilting threads also set the sections apart. Where the paws interlock, I quilted around the paws to outline them.

Quilt design ideas

The finished block is 9" square. You can, of course, draft this block to any size and possibly use several sizes in the same quilt. Any one of numerous settings could be tried. Using both traditional Bear's Paw blocks and Paw Within Paw blocks together might be a good idea, or you might use a different color for each of the three bears: baby, mama, and papa. The small pieces make this pattern ideal for using up your small scraps. Quilting circles on the toes and pads of the feet might be fun to try.

BEAR COUNTRY details: appliquéd bears.

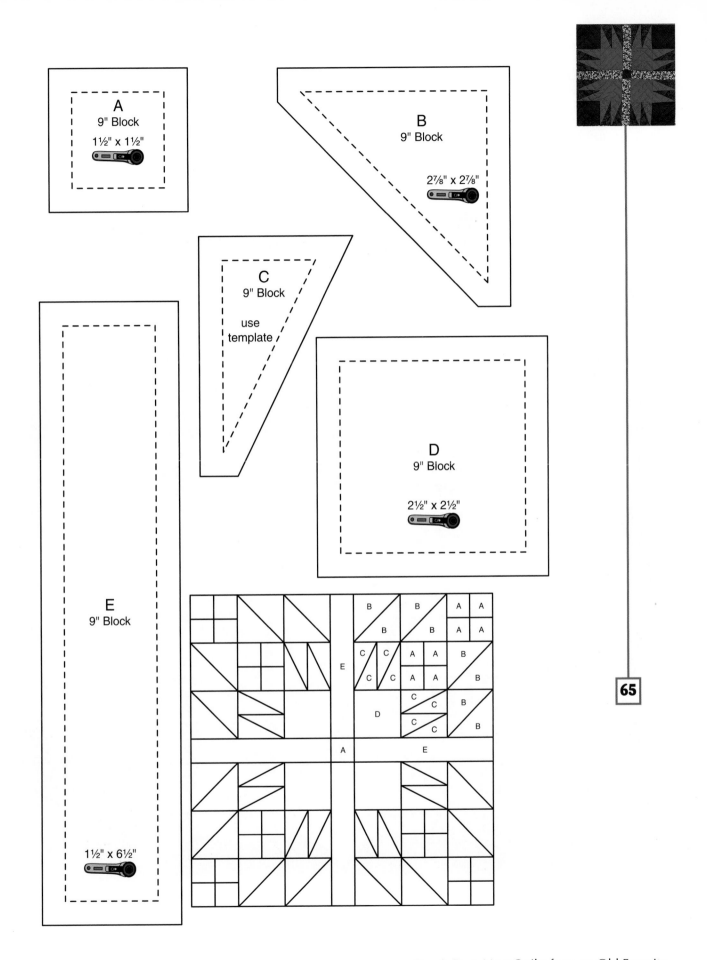

A
9" Block
1½" x 1½"

B
9" Block
2⅞" x 2⅞"

C
9" Block
use template

D
9" Block
2½" x 2½"

E
9" Block
1½" x 6½"

B		B		A	A
B		B		A	A
C	C	A	A		B
C	C	A	A		B
		C		C		B
		C		C		B

E

D

A

E

65

Bear's Paw: New Quilts from an Old Favorite

Oblique

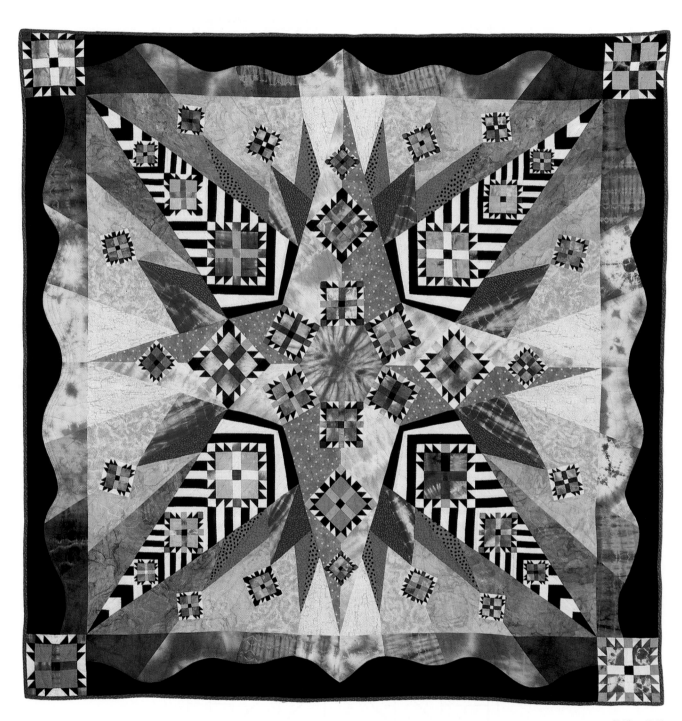

74" x 74"

Bear's Paw: New Quilts from an Old Favorite

I n addition to quiltmaking, I enjoy designing machine knitting patterns and wearable arts.

Meet the quilter

The sewing machine was always an important part of my early years. Watching my mother sew and having her teach me to make my own clothing at an early age was the groundwork for my quilting, which began some 30 years ago.

Some of my earliest memories were of color: playing with buttons, colored paper, or fabric scraps. Working with color is what keeps me coming back. The excitement I feel, whenever an idea actually takes shape in a sketch and then in fabric, gratifies my desire for creative achievement.

Around 1980, a couple of quilts by Maria McCormick-Snyder, CHRYSALIS: LOG CABIN VARIATION III and LOG CABIN IV, were published in a magazine. Those beautiful quilts were very exciting, and I found myself returning to the pictures again and again to study those great works of art. They were the inspiration for me to begin stepping outside the lines of tradition. Many of my quilts have been developed from the old patterns used in a contemporary manner.

A great deal of my time is spent experimenting and making small samples. Many of my fabrics are hand dyed because of all the color possibilities that can be produced. I am beginning to experiment with potato and corn dextrin, hoping for some interesting textures and happenings. A recent quilt was hand quilted in a week with many colors of pearl cotton and embroidery floss in a large, primitive stitch. Sometimes it is fun to break the rules.

Inspiration and design

After having at least a dozen ideas for a Bear's Paw quilt, I still felt that none of them was just right. Over coffee one morning, I drew up a new idea in a small thumbnail sketch that made me want to get out my fabric and start sewing. I drew one-fourth of the design full-sized on heavy paper to use for a master pattern, then made freezer-paper templates from the master drawing.

Bear's Paw: New Quilts from an Old Favorite

Several Bear's Paw blocks were made up in black, white, and gray and placed on the design wall for further study. Colors were added and subtracted until they were pleasing. After making the center portion and placing it on wall, I decided it needed a border, and choosing black to give the eye a place to stop seemed just the thing.

Drafting blocks any size

To break free of traditional block settings, it's helpful to know how to draft blocks in any size. The following drafting technique is easy to do and can be used for any block that can be drawn on a grid.

• Draw a square the size you need for your block. For this example, we will use a 10" Bear's Paw block.

• You will need seven equal divisions for a Bear's Paw block. On your ruler, find a number divisible by 7 that is greater than the size of the block. In the example, that would be 14".

• Lay the ruler so that the "0" is at the lower-left corner. Place the 14" mark on the right side of the block. (For block sizes in which the measurement is too large to fit inside the block, extend the right side of the block as needed.)

• Mark a dot every 2" along the ruler. Using a triangle placed along the bottom edge of the square, draw the lines to make seven divisions.

• Rotate the paper a quarter turn and repeat the process to complete the grid.

• With your ruler and a fine pen, draw the block on the grid.

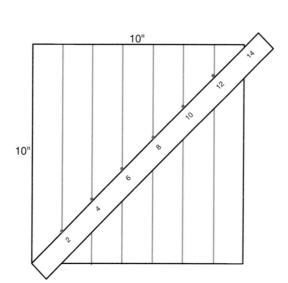
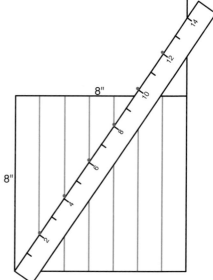

Method for drawing a grid on any size block.

Bear's Paw: New Quilts from an Old Favorite

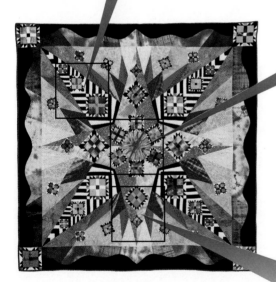

Bear's Paw: New Quilts from an Old Favorite

Bear Necessity

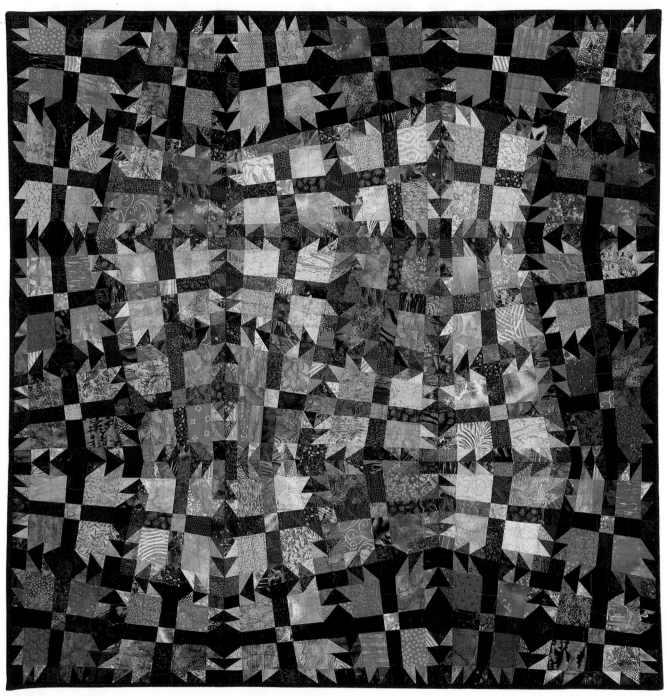

53" x 53"

Bear's Paw: New Quilts from an Old Favorite

Quilting is a wonderful medium because I can make something original even though I'm not good at drawing or painting.

Meet the quilter

I became a quilter almost reluctantly, trying a variety of handwork techniques to make gifts for friends and family. Eventually, I realized I could probably make a quilt with all my new skills, so I made a lap-sized sampler and was hooked.

Early on, I was taught the love of multi-fabric quilts, the value of value, and the skill of accurate piecing. Today, I enjoy using my computer to design quilts and to make decorative quilt labels with clip art and fancy fonts.

Currently, I am using foundation paper piecing. It's amazing how many intricate pictorial designs are possible with this technique. I am so grateful to all those talented designers who shared their wonderful realistic and incredibly detailed patterns with us. At the same time, I am grateful for the traditional geometric patterns in our quilting heritage. We are truly blessed to have so many choices for fulfilling our need to create.

Inspiration and design

BEAR NECESSITY was inspired by the annual MAQS contest. I have entered the contest each year for five years now. I like the challenge of interpreting a traditional pattern and trying to disguise the original pattern source.

My previous quilts were based on blocks that were not square, resulting in quilts with uneven edges. This time, I used a skewed grid within a square block, resulting in a square, even-edged quilt. I designed the piece with computer quilting software. It was a challenge figuring out how to draw a seven-patch pattern in a skewed grid on the computer, but the resulting accuracy was worth the effort. Also, once the block was drawn, the coloring process was much easier and faster.

After the quilt was designed, I printed a master copy of the block. To reproduce the foundations, I layered this master with several sheets of freezer paper and sewed over the lines on the sewing machine with an unthreaded needle. These patterns were then cut into units that could be foun-

71

dation paper pieced on the machine. Foundations greatly simplified the piecing of this block, because all the pieces were different sizes.

I like to make multi-fabric quilts and to work with a value change between the border and the center. It requires a lot of fabric to achieve this look, and there are more than 150 fabrics in BEAR NECESSITY. It is machine quilted with numerous cotton threads in colors that match the fabrics. For the backing, I pieced a large traditional Bear's Paw block from the same fabrics used for the quilt.

Skewed Bear's Paw Block

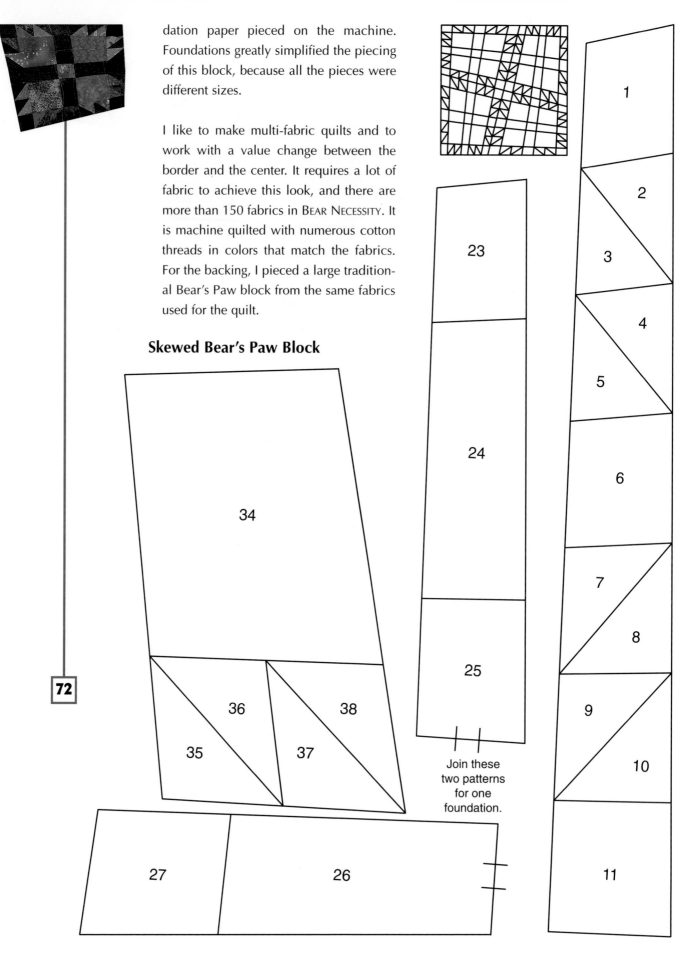

Join these two patterns for one foundation.

Bear's Paw: New Quilts from an Old Favorite

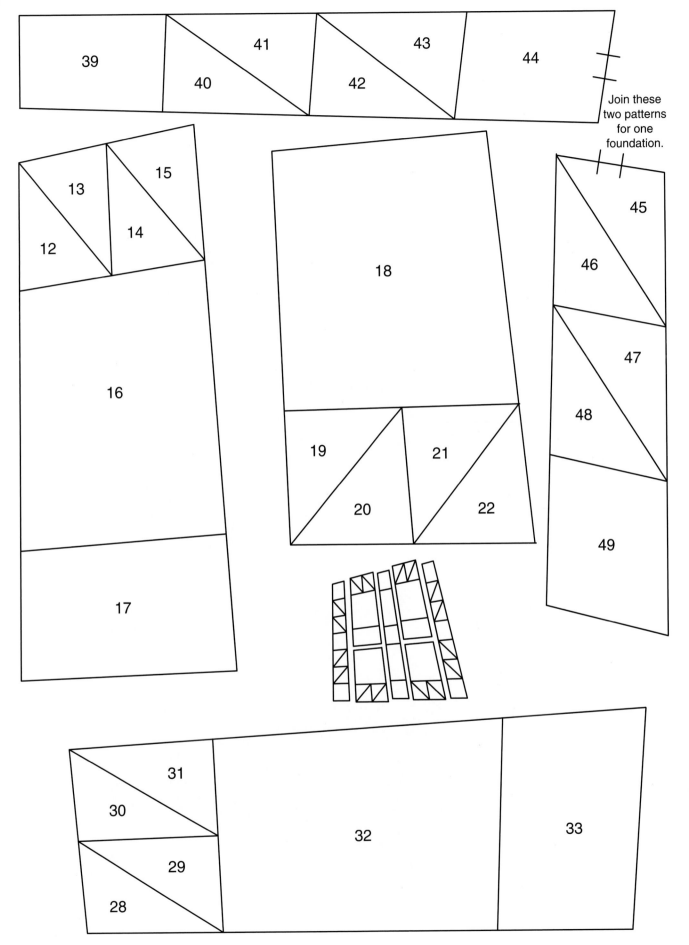

39

41

40

43

42

44

Join these
two patterns
for one
foundation.

13

15

14

12

18

16

45

46

47

48

19

21

20

22

49

17

31

30

29

32

33

28

Bear's Paw: New Quilts from an Old Favorite

Investment Journey

64" x 86"

Bear's Paw: New Quilts from an Old Favorite

STASH Group
Left to right, back row: Jan Krakenberg, Terri Jacobson, Stephanie Muehlhausen,
Carol Wheeler, Jean Van Bockel, Gayle Noyes.
Center row: Judy Siegford, Lois Grutta, Kim Erk, Sally Clouse, Nola Mauch, Sharon Gilman.
Front row: Jo Shoemaker, Betty Franzatti, Nancy Criswell, Terry Miller, Thine Bloxham.
Not pictured: Rebecca Scribner, Carol Bean.

T his quilt represents a collaborative effort by the Silver Thimbles
and Stock Holdings (STASH) investment and quilting group.
It symbolizes the group's investing journey.

Meet the quilters

The idea for a group was the inspiration of Jo Shoemaker, who was trying to invest her early
retirement package. After talking to stock brokers and researching trading techniques, stocks,
and mutual funds, she felt overwhelmed and realized she had a lot to learn. Who better to
learn with than fellow quilters?

The idea of an all-female, all-quilter investment club generated interest among her friends in
the North Idaho Quilters. In April 1997, our group was founded with 16 members from the
Coeur d'Alene, Idaho, area. We share a life-long interest in fabric, design, and sewing, as well
as a dedication to learning. Many of the members have been quilting for as long as 28 years.
Some have careers, others have had careers, and all lead busy lives. A mix of backgrounds,
ages, occupations, and interests makes our group dynamic and exciting. We call the group
STASH, which has two meanings. One signifies the hope of earning a stash of money, and the
other a stash of quilt fabric.

We began setting goals for learning about the stock market and planning investments. At
monthly 7:00 A.M. meetings stocks are discussed, a financial report is given, and something of
interest about investing is provided. Three members meet more frequently to select stocks to
study for potential investing. The group follows the National Association of Investors
Corporation guidelines for learning and occasionally has a financial expert as a guest speak-
er. However, most of what we learn is self taught. We study Value Line and read books and
magazines on investing to learn about the stocks we buy.

Bear's Paw: New Quilts from an Old Favorite

The all-female group creates a comfortable learning environment. If we don't know something, we ask or research the topic. Our comfort levels with investing have increased to where many members are investing on their own as well as with the group. Our portfolio is diverse and includes established companies. The goal is to double our money by our five-year anniversary.

The members

Carol Bean has been quilting for 20 years. She is a retired nurse and college professor and does accounting for her husband's business.

Thine Bloxham made her first quilt in high school and has been quilting seriously for 15 years. She owns Timber Lane Press, a pattern publishing company.

Sally Clouse has been quilting about 18 years. She is a homemaker and past president of North Idaho quilters.

Nancy Criswell began quilting at her mother's side. Her mother and grandmother were her inspirations. She has been in a quilt group that has met weekly for 20 years.

Kim Erk began quilting in the 70s but only learned precision piecing in the 90s. The thrill of quilting came through to her after a quilt she had participated in making won a blue ribbon. It is a great diversion from her career as a civil engineer technician.

Betty Franzatti began quilting in 1974, has been teaching quilting since 1980, and does consignment and photo-transfer quilts.

Sharon Gilman has been quilting for about 10 years. She is retired after working as a sales clerk and bookkeeper.

Lois Grutta began quilting in 1984. She helped organize the first Quilt San Diego and later the Michigan Quilt Network.

Terri Jacobson has been quilting for 18 years and is a homemaker and student.

Jan Krakenberg has been quilting for 10 years, but she never has enough time because she works full time in the medical field.

Nola Mauch became a quilter eight years ago. Since then, all her other crafts are in a drawer, probably never to be done.

Terry Miller has been quilting 16 years and is a retired home economics teacher and school secretary.

Stephanie Muehlhausen has been quilting for 22 years and is the owner of A Stitch in Time, a local quilt shop.

Gayle Noyes has been quilting for 28 years. She works and teaches at A Stitch in Time.

Rebecca Scribner has been quilting for three years and made her first quilt at age 25. She is a new mother and works in the dental field.

Jo Shoemaker made her first quilt at age 16. She is the owner of a small garden nursery with her daughter.

Judy Siegford began quilting seven years ago. She worked as the office manager in a dental clinic and is now retired.

Jean Van Bockel has been quilting for about 14 years. She works and teaches at A Stitch in Time quilt shop.

Carol Wheeler began quilting in the 70s. She and two partners owned the Log Cabin Dry Goods quilt shop. Now, she enjoys belonging to quilt groups and finishing her own projects.

76

Inspiration and design

The quilt idea began after a particularly difficult study session. The group was perplexed and discouraged over a difficult investment concept, when someone mentioned making a quilt about investing. This brought the group to life immediately. At the next meeting, suggestions were discussed, and the best ideas were combined in the final design.

The INVESTMENT JOURNEY quilt is a collaborative work symbolizing our journey to learn about stock-market investing. The brick background signifies stability and sound investment planning. The 16 members are featured sitting around a smaller quilt and working together to make learning and quilting easy and fun. The smaller center quilt shows a bull charging down the investment path, stomping on small Bear's Paw blocks as he goes. Baskets filled with golden eggs remind us not to put all our eggs in one basket. The "blue sky" behind the skyline and the New York Stock Exchange shows an investment world filled with opportunity. The quilt has very little red, because the group wants to stay in the black.

We decided to use our own body shapes for the figures set around the smaller quilt. To achieve the unique perspective looking down at the group, we took 35-mm slides from the loft of a barn. We sat around a table and the photographer took separate slides of each side of the table.

Later the slides were projected on a wall so that we were able to reduce the actual body sizes by half. Body outlines and details were traced on freezer paper. These original tracings were copied so each member had one copy of their body for reference and another to use as a pattern. Each person designed her own outfit,

chose hair fabric similar to her real hair color, and appliquéd her pieces together.

If this is something you would like to try, we recommend planning a photo shoot so there is good contrast between the subjects' clothing and hair and the backgrounds. The contrast is helpful for accuracy when tracing patterns.

All sections of the quilt were worked on at the same time. Some group members pieced the background, others planned the road, the bull, and the skyline. To assemble the quilt top, the small center quilt and the benches were machine top stitched over the brick background with long basting stitches. The people were placed around the center quilt and hand appliquéd in place. The visible edges of the small center quilt and benches were hand appliquéd, and the remaining basting stitches were removed. The quilt was quilted by hand and machine.

Quilting is a major part of all of our lives, but it is challenging to do a group project with 16 people. We may wait awhile to attempt this again. Who knows when a new problem or idea will inspire us once more.

INVESTMENT JOURNEY detail

Bear's Paw: New Quilts from an Old Favorite

Sunpaw

50" x 54"

Bear's Paw: New Quilts from an Old Favorite

Cherie St. Cyr   Susan Marks

In this collaboration, Cherie made most of the cloth and did the quilting. Susan did the piecing and embellishing.

Meet the quilters

Cherie St. Cyr: Quilting was an accident that snuck up on me through the backdoor of painting. My sister, who was watching me paint at my mother's table one summer, said, "Why don't you sew all those cute little silk paintings together and have cousin Jean quilt them?" As someone who was sewing-impaired, I certainly wasn't going to do it. I did pack a rather large piece off to cousin Jean and got back an impressive wallhanging. Nine years later, I sit in my studio with thousands of dollars worth of sewing machines and millions of yards of hand–dyed and painted cloth and wonder about innocent questions from well-intentioned sisters.

My great love is textile design. I use a variety of non-toxic resists, such as sugars from corn and potato, cassava paste, and sulfites to do odd and miraculous things to cloth. In SUNPAW, the crackle pattern was made with potato dextrin.

Susan and I met at a quilt club meeting, and we were the only two using nontraditional techniques. I asked her to collaborate on a piece for the MAQS competition. We immediately began working on two pieces and voted on the one we would finish for the slides.

I always work on 10 to 15 pieces at a time. My design walls are often in need of an archeologist to find where my brain has been and is going. Currently, I am working on some collaborative pieces with other painters. A lovely velveteen quilt is nearing completion. The

79

centerpiece was discharged (bleached patterns) by a fellow painter, then over-painted and pieced.

In the assembly process, I usually start with a painting I really like and pull supporting textiles from my stash. It often amazes me that some cloth I painted and really don't like will be perfect in a certain situation. When piecing a top, I rarely use a straight edge and never mark a quilting pattern, rather I use my sewing machine like a pencil, drawing free-form and sometimes funky patterns. I work in my studio 40 hours a week and sell my quilts at art fairs.

Susan Marks: I've always done textile-related things. I knitted and crocheted as a child but was something of a disaster when it came to sewing clothing. About five years ago, I discovered the joy of creating my own needlepoint designs, but the execution was a little slow for my busy life. During something of a crisis in my professional life, I discovered an art camp where I spent a glorious week learning some free methods of hand quilting and embellishing. I've never turned back.

Quilts and textiles give me great joy. After a lifetime of searching, I have finally found my medium of self-expression. I like how quilts are built in layers and the entire design doesn't have to be preconceived. My life has become very rich, filled with more ideas for quilts than there is time to make them. As a bonus, I enjoy the warm community and bond shared easily with other quilters and explorers of textile art.

For my other projects, I'd like to complete the other Bear's Paw quilt, already started and hanging lonely on the design wall. I'm also working on an appliquéd quilt

based on STARS IN THE GARDEN by Becky Goldsmith and Linda Jenkins. My quilt is set with random stripes and triangle borders. I'm also starting a small piece in a series of alter images and using a lot of what I call contemporary English embroidery.

I like to work on more than one thing at a time. Yes, I know we should finish things and I actually do finish about 90 percent of my projects, but if there's just one thing in progress, I get stuck, frustrated, and unhappy. My friend Susie Shie once told me, "Have more things going, girl. Then when you get stuck, just switch to one of the others. That little space in your brain will quietly figure out what to do on the first one, and meanwhile, you'll be finishing two pieces!"

Inspiration and design

The quilt was made almost exclusively with fabrics created by Cherie. The fabrics themselves directed the design. Random and curve piecing were used throughout, arriving at a quilt without a single straight line of stitching.

Cherie has entered many quilt contests, but this was my first. The inspiration came from the central panel, which I cut into four sections and inserted navy fabric through those cuts. From there, the red paws (done with potato dextrin) on the gold seemed obvious. After the flower or sun design appeared, some green ground seemed to be needed, and thus the quilt took shape.

Potato-dextrin resist

This lovely nontoxic resist was discovered by Jason Pollen, president of the Surface Design Association. He tested 800 different starches as he looked for interesting design possibilities.

Bear's Paw: New Quilts from an Old Favorite

Recipe

1 C boiling water
1⅓ C potato dextrin

Add the potato dextrin to the boiling water and beat with a hand mixer until it is white and creamy like frosting. Let the mixture cool a bit, then apply it to stretched cloth that has been soaked in a soda-ash solution. Allow the cloth to dry.

When cracks appear (the time varies with the heat and humidity), apply thickened dye. Cover the piece with plastic for 4–24 hours. Wash.

Sources of potato dextrin:

Pro Chemical & Dye, Inc.

P.O. Box 14, Somerset, MA 02726
phone: 508-76-3838
        800-2buy-dye (orders only)
fax: 508-676-3980
e-mail: pro-chemical@worldnet.att.net
web page: www.prochemical.com

Dharma Trading Co.

P.O. Box 150916, San Rafael, CA 94915
phone: 415-456-7657
        800-542-5227 (orders only)
fax: 415-456-8747
e-mail: catalog@dharmatrading.com
web page: www.djarmatrading.com

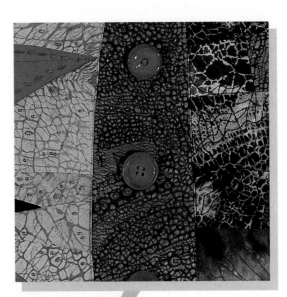

Bear's Paw: New Quilts from an Old Favorite

Brown Bear

66" x 80"

Bear's Paw: New Quilts from an Old Favorite

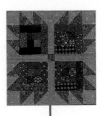

Joan Walker Oregon City, OR

This quilt has a wool batting and is hand quilted. I consider this relaxation my reward after many miles at the sewing machine.

Meet the quilter

After years of admiring quilts, I began quiltmaking in 1993 when my husband uttered those fateful words, "Couldn't you make one of those?" Being an admirer of Amish quilts, I started with a 120"-square, hand-quilted, Amish center-diamond pattern. It quickly became apparent that a class was in order. Many, many classes later, I found quilting to be a wonderful hobby and the friends made along the way to be very important in my life.

It seems that, no matter how hard the day, you can always take a mental break by letting your mind drift to quilt designs. I find myself much more aware of my surroundings, their colors and designs, with each new project. I make quilts for the wonderful serenity it brings to my life, for the friendship and camaraderie that is inherent in the quilt world, and for the opportunity to travel in a world of simplicity, gentleness, and friendship.

I remember watching my mother's enjoyment while sewing. She was an avid seamstress, who passed away many years before the quilt bug hit me in middle age. As a child, I disliked sewing so much that, to pass my high school home economics class, I actually paid my best friend to sew all of my homework. Now I've gone from paying someone to sew for me to spending most of my discretionary income on classes, supplies, and fabrics. I'm fortunate to have a supportive husband who is also very helpful during the design process.

Quilt shows provide a wonderful opportunity to learn and share, and to be inspired and challenged (and to buy cool fabric with friends at the vendor mall). BROWN BEAR is the first quilt I have ever entered in a show. It has been a tremendous joy because it has been honored by winning our local annual quilt show and by being juried into The Association of Pacific Northwest Quilters semi-annual show, and by being selected as a finalist in this MAQS contest. Quilt shows are such a wonderful celebration of the work of all quiltmakers.

Inspiration and design

I wanted to make a masculine quilt that my husband, Charlie, would enjoy and that reflected the beautiful colors of the Native American baskets and textiles we both love. The scrappy nature of the pattern appealed to me because it meant a lot of fabric could be used.

The quilt is machine pieced with all-cotton fabrics in a subtle, muted palette. A gem-tone quilt had preceded this one, and muted colors were calling to me. I like to construct one block at a time and then have it tell me what should come next. I don't normally start a project with a preconceived notion of the borders, sashing, quilting pattern, or even the finished size, other than wall or bed quilts. Experience has taught me that my preconceptions are usually wrong.

I have always enjoyed the new and innovative versions of traditional patterns that are the hallmark of the MAQS contest. While BROWN BEAR is firmly based in tradition, with only a slight twist, I enjoy the simplicity of combining the two classic patterns, the Bear's Paw and a Log Cabin. This breaking up of a block is easily applicable to many traditional patterns.

As for the quilting, I wish I had started wearing glasses *before* hand quilting this quilt, rather than after. What a difference! I almost doubled my stitches per inch on the next quilt, by wearing an inexpensive pair of glasses from the grocery store.

Brown Bear Wall Quilt Pattern

19½" finished size

Here is a suggestion for an easy project – frame a quilt block. If you have leftover blocks, attach one or two borders and frame the piece as art. The block in the photo is quilted, but you could leave yours unquilted if you desire. It was an extra block from BROWN BEAR. Its colors didn't fit into the quilt, but on its own, it worked well.

For framing, add approximately 3" all around for attaching the block to the back of a mat board. I had this block professionally framed because it is not a standard size, but you could make a block to fit a standard frame and frame it yourself. You could even bypass the borders and let a mat or two do the work for you.

Sashing and Borders

J	1¾" x 13½"	cut 4
K	1" x 16"	cut 2
L	1" x 17"	cut 2
M	2" x 17"	cut 2
N	2" x 20"	cut 2

13" Log Cabin Bear's Paw Block

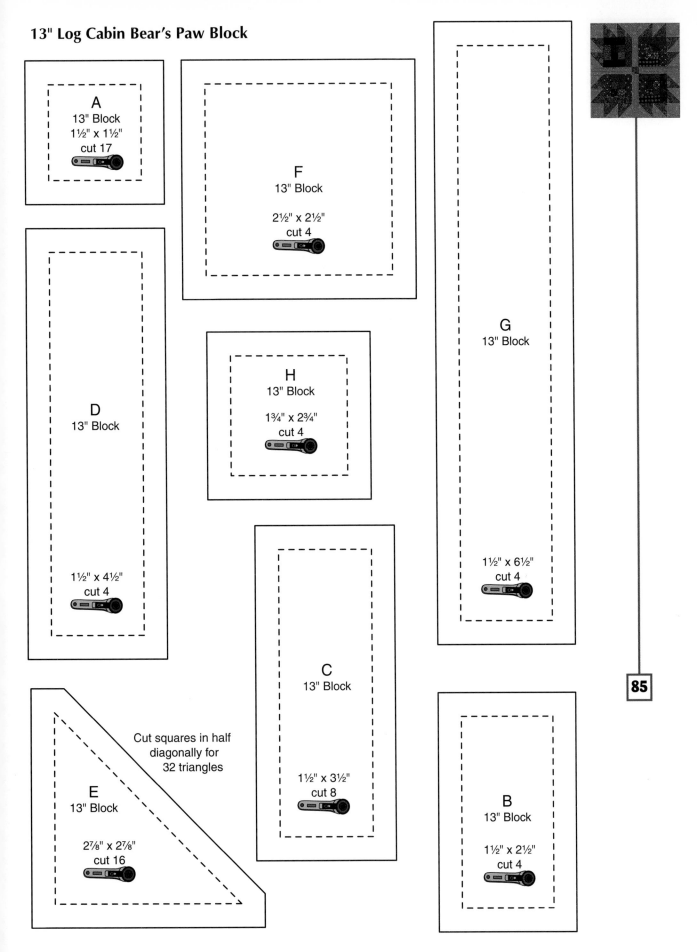

A
13" Block
1½" x 1½"
cut 17

F
13" Block
2½" x 2½"
cut 4

H
13" Block
1¾" x 2¾"
cut 4

D
13" Block
1½" x 4½"
cut 4

G
13" Block
1½" x 6½"
cut 4

E
13" Block
Cut squares in half diagonally for 32 triangles
2⅞" x 2⅞"
cut 16

C
13" Block
1½" x 3½"
cut 8

B
13" Block
1½" x 2½"
cut 4

85

Bear's Paw: New Quilts from an Old Favorite

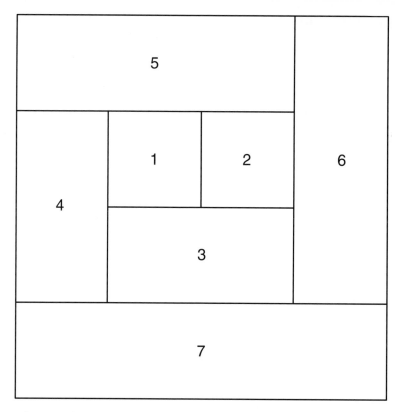

If you prefer to paper foundation piece the Log Cabin centers of the blocks, you can use this pattern. Notice that it has only three fabrics in the center instead of four A's.

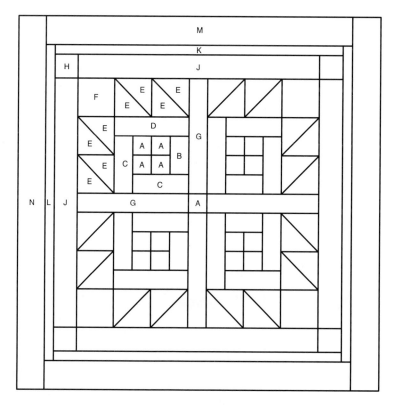

Quilt assembly

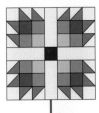

More Bear's Paw Blocks

The Bear's Paw block is known by several names, including Bear's Foot and Cat's Paw. The *Encyclopedia of Pieced Quilt Patterns*, by Barbara Brackman, shows a 1932 variation of the block in which the largest square is divided into four squares. In another block by the same name, the paw has six claws, and four of the paws are rotated pinwheel-fashion.

For your piecing pleasure, we have included full-sized templates for all three blocks in several sizes. If you need a size we have not given, see Elizabeth Rymer's description for drafting blocks in any size on page 68.

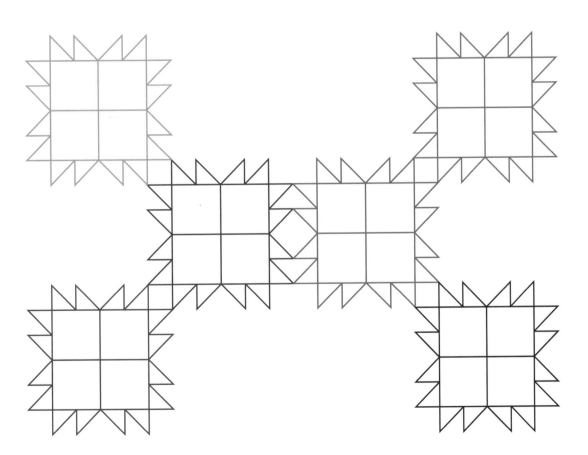

Bear's Paw: New Quilts from an Old Favorite

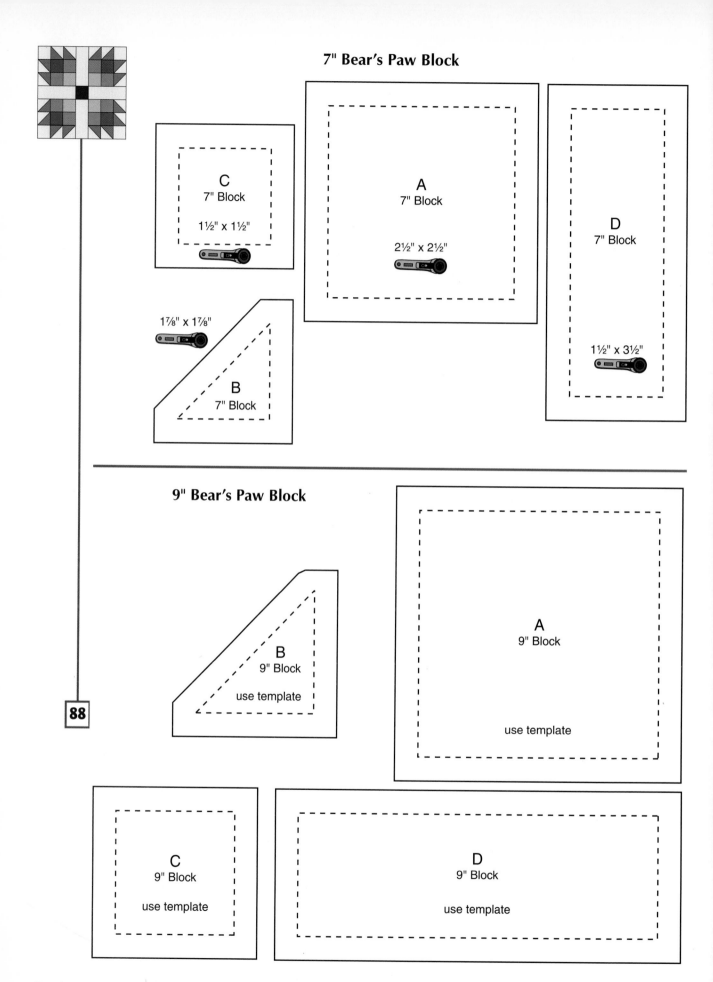

7" Bear's Paw Block

C
7" Block

1½" x 1½"

A
7" Block

2½" x 2½"

D
7" Block

1½" x 3½"

1⅞" x 1⅞"

B
7" Block

9" Bear's Paw Block

B
9" Block

use template

A
9" Block

use template

C
9" Block

use template

D
9" Block

use template

88

Bear's Paw: New Quilts from an Old Favorite

10½" Bear's Paw Block

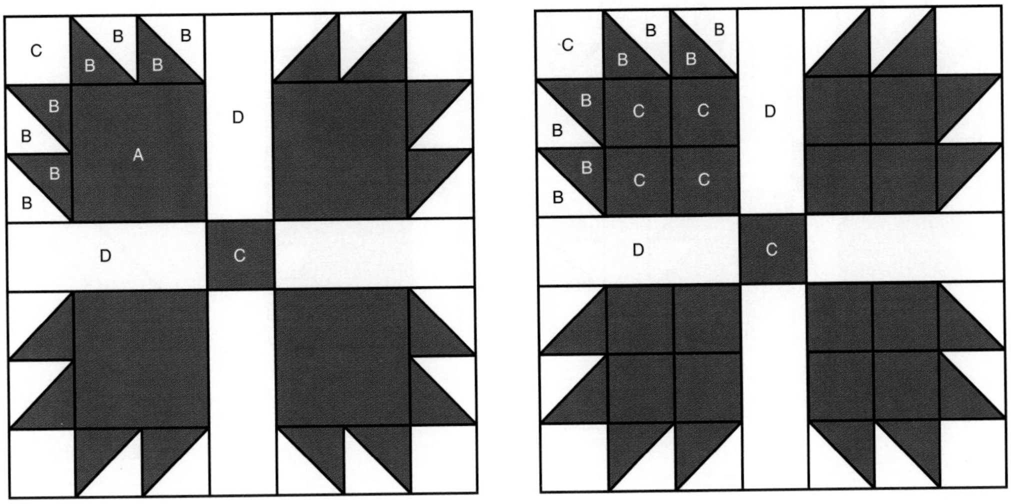

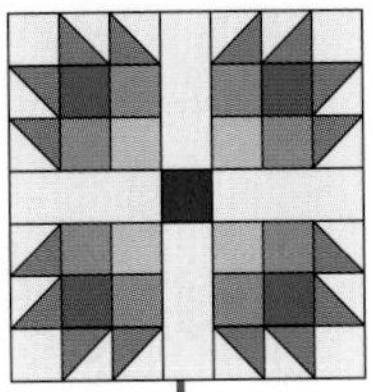

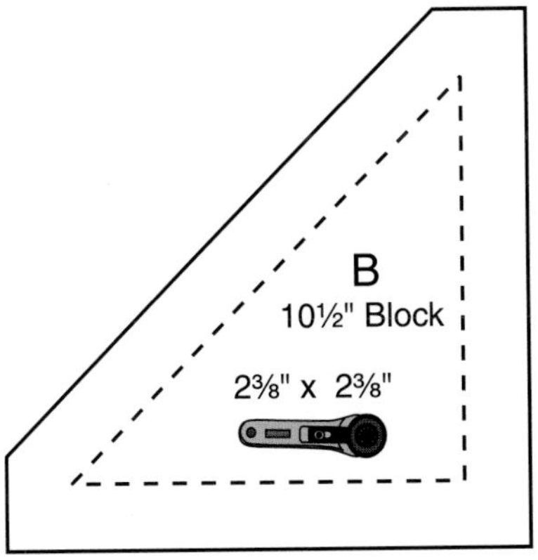

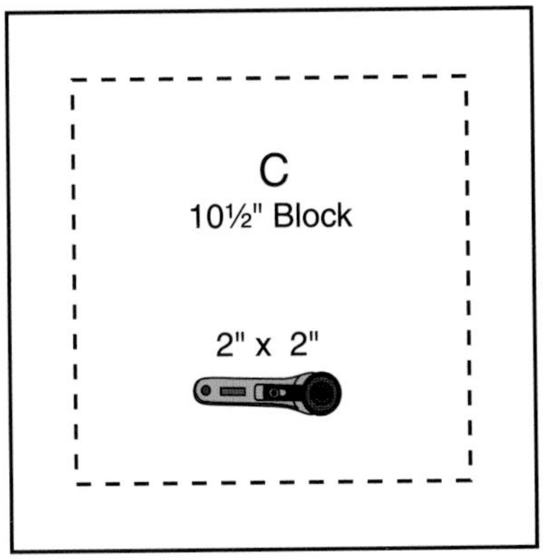

B
10½" Block

2⅜" x 2⅜"

C
10½" Block

2" x 2"

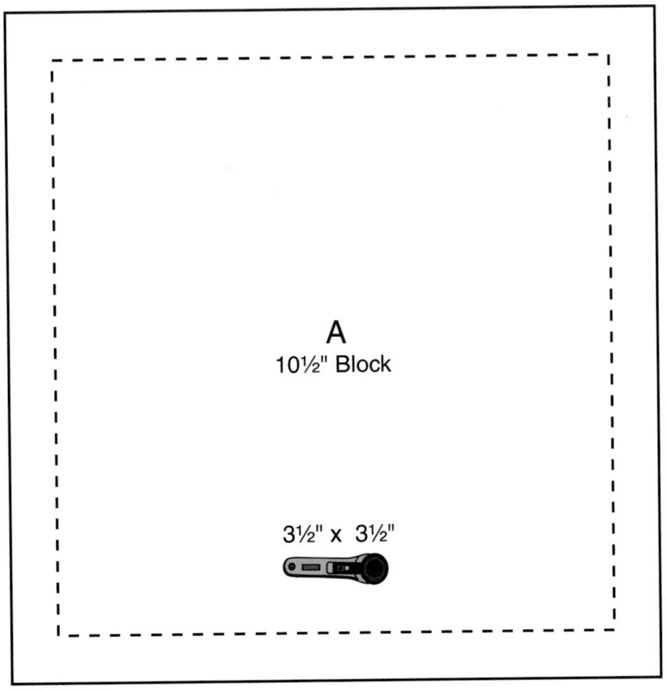

A
10½" Block

3½" x 3½"

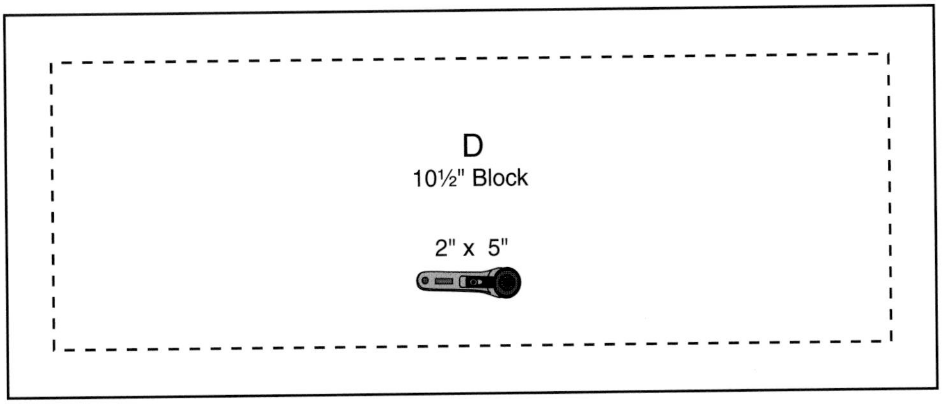

D
10½" Block

2" x 5"

89

Bear's Paw: New Quilts from an Old Favorite

12" Bear's Paw Block

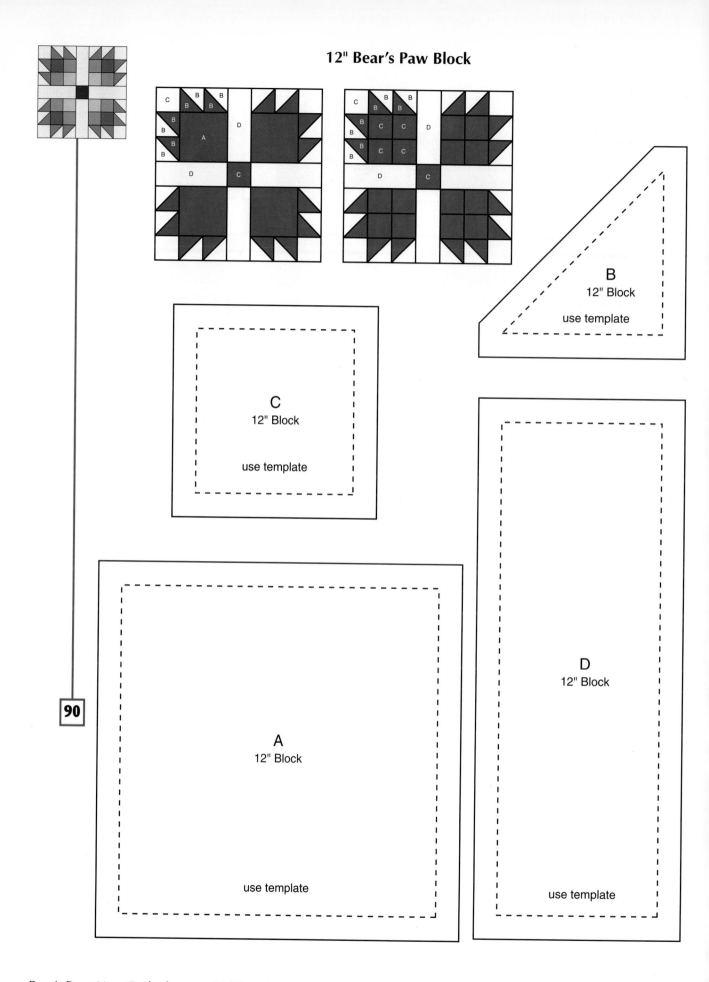

C
12" Block

use template

B
12" Block

use template

A
12" Block

use template

D
12" Block

use template

90

Bear's Paw: New Quilts from an Old Favorite

Possible Block Variations

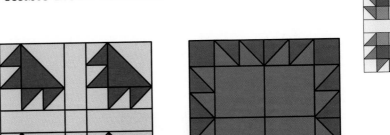

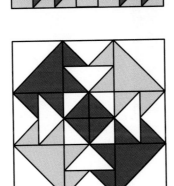

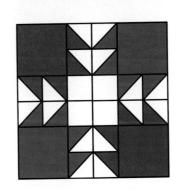

8" Bear's Paw Variation

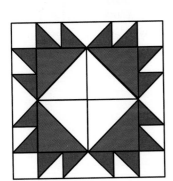

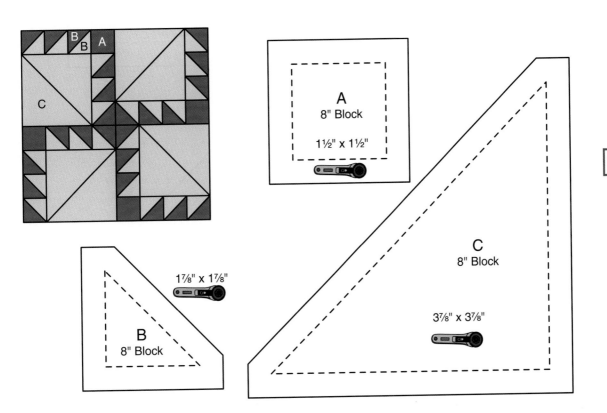

B
B A

C

A
8" Block

1½" x 1½"

B
8" Block

1⅞" x 1⅞"

C
8" Block

3⅞" x 3⅞"

Bear's Paw: New Quilts from an Old Favorite

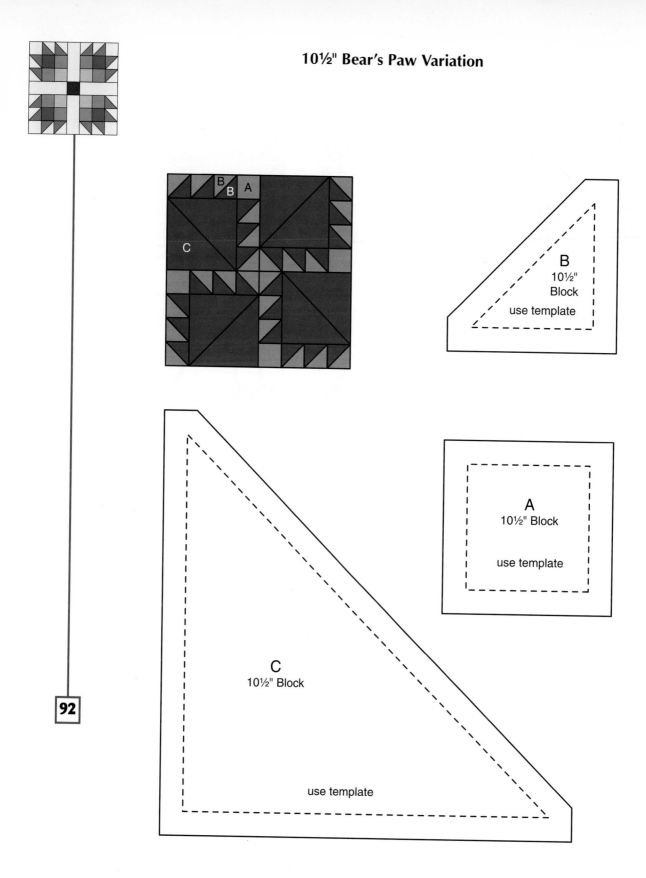

Bear's Paw: New Quilts from an Old Favorite

14" Bear's Paw Variation

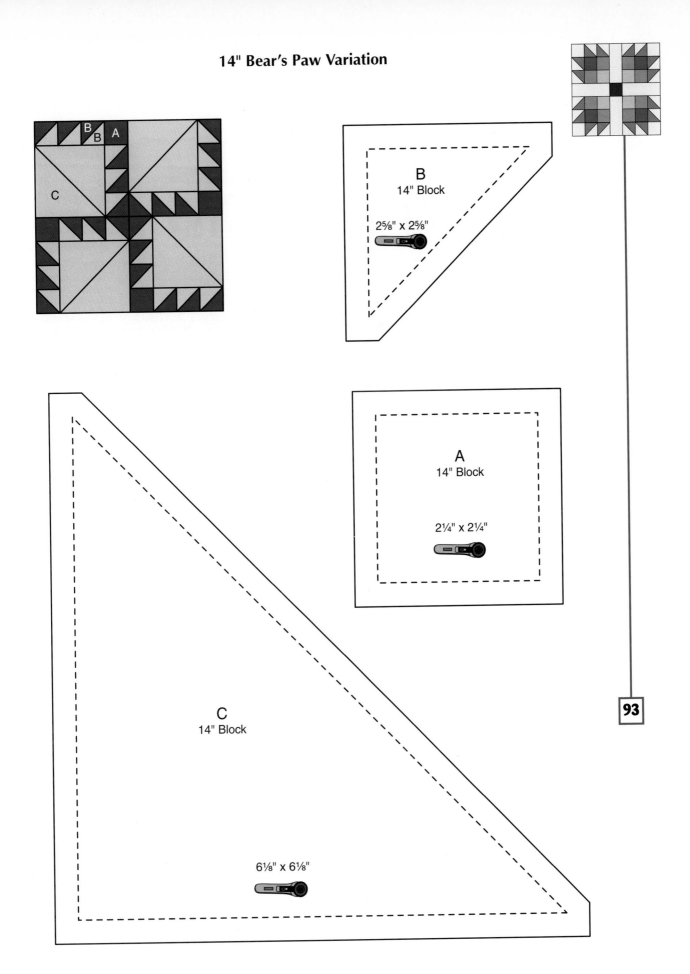

B
14" Block

2⅝" x 2⅝"

A
14" Block

2¼" x 2¼"

C
14" Block

6⅛" x 6⅛"

93

94

The Museum of the American Quilter's Society (MAQS) is an exciting place where the public can learn more about quilts, quiltmaking, and quiltmakers. Founded in 1991 by Bill and Meredith Schroeder as a not-for-profit organization, MAQS is located in an expansive 27,000 square-foot facility, making it the largest quilt museum in the world. Its facility includes three exhibit galleries, four class-rooms, and a gift and book shop.

Through collecting quilts and other programs, MAQS focuses on celebrating and developing today's quiltmaking. It also provides a comprehensive program of exhibits, activities, events, and services to educate about the ever-developing art and tradition of quiltmaking. Whether presenting new or antique quilts, MAQS promotes understanding of, and respect for, all quilts – new and antique, tradi-tional and innovative, machine made and hand made, utility and art.

The MAQS exhibit galleries regularly feature a selection of the Museum's own collection of quilts made from the 1980s on, as well as exhibits of new and antique quilts and related archival materials. Workshops, conferences, and exhib-it-related publications provide additional educational opportunities. The Museum's shop carries a wide selection of fine crafts and hundreds of quilt and textile books.

Located in historic downtown Paducah, Kentucky, MAQS is open year-round 10 A.M. to 5 P.M. Monday through Saturday. From April 1 through October 31, it is also open on Sundays from 1–5 P.M. The entire facility is wheelchair accessible.

MAQS programs can also be enjoyed on the website: www.quiltmuseum.org or through MAQS traveling exhibits like the annual *New Quilts from an Old Favorites* contest and exhibit. For more information, write MAQS, PO Box 1540, Paducah, KY 42002-1540; phone (270) 442-8856; email info@quiltmuseum.org.

Bear's Paw: New Quilts from an Old Favorite

OTHER AQS BOOKS

AQS books are known worldwide for timely topics, clear writing, beautiful color photos, and accurate illustrations and patterns. This is only a small selection of the books available from your local bookseller, quilt shop, or public library.

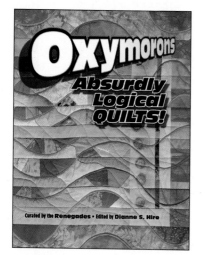

#5753   US $19.95

#4627   US $16.95

#5098   US $16.95

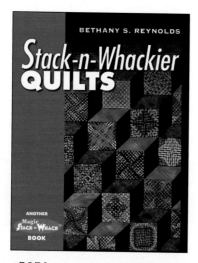

#5850   Fall 2001

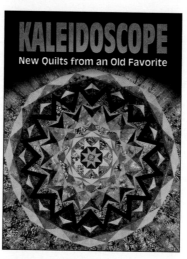

#5296   US $16.95

#5592   US $19.95

#5744   US $9.95

#5590   US $24.95

#4911   US $16.95

Look for these books nationally or call **1-800-626-5420**